TO THE STUDENT

The Poetry Processor gives you the chance to explore poetry, to write poems yourself, and to read and enjoy poems written by other people.

Poetry is powerful.

- Poetry can help you to use words more skilfully and imaginatively
- Poetry can help you to find pleasure in words
  - in their music, through rhythm, rhyme and sound
  - in their meanings, through wordplay and riddles
  - in their pattern, through the way they join together to make a whole poem
- Poetry can be a way of speaking about things that matter to you
- Poetry can make you more aware of the world around you
- Poetry can help you to discover things about yourself and other people.
- Poetry can challenge, shock, provoke and surprise.

This book shows you some of the many different types of poetry that you can find, and that you can write anytime, anywhere.

Paul Higgins.

1 BALLADS

A ballad is a rhyming poem which tells a story. The story is often violent or tragic.

In the days before television, radio and even newspapers, when most people could not read or write, ballads were a familiar form of entertainment. They were also a way of spreading news; and just as with our Sunday papers, murders and scandals were always popular material.

Ballads are meant to be spoken or sung. The ballad is an oral form of poetry, so the sound of the words is particularly important.

Read the following ballad aloud in pairs or small groups.

THE BALLAD OF CHARLOTTE DYMOND   Charles Causley

Charlotte Dymond, a domestic servant aged eighteen, was murdered near Rowtor Ford on Bodmin Moor on Sunday, 14 April 1844, by her young man, a crippled farm-hand, Matthew Weeks, aged twenty-two. A stone marks the spot.

It was a Sunday evening
   And in the April rain
That Charlotte went from our house
   And never came home again.

Her shawl of diamond redcloth,
   She wore a yellow gown,
She carried the green gauze handkerchief
   She bought in Bodmin town.

About her throat her necklace
   And in her purse her pay:
The four silver shillings
   She had at Lady Day.

In her purse four shillings
   And in her purse her pride
As she walked out one evening
   Her lover at her side.

Out beyond the marshes
   Where the cattle stand,
With her crippled lover
   Limping at her hand.

Charlotte walked with Matthew
  Through the Sunday mist,
Never saw the razor
  Waiting at his wrist.

Charlotte she was gentle
  But they found her in the flood
Her Sunday beads among the reeds
  Beaming with her blood

Matthew where is Charlotte,
  And wherefore has she flown?
For you walked out together
  And now are come alone.

Why do you not answer,
  Stand silent as a tree,
Your Sunday worsted stockings
  All muddied to the knee?

Why do you mend your breast-pleat
  With a rusty needle's thread
And fall with fears and silent tears
  Upon your single bed?

Why do you sit so sadly
  Your face the colour of clay
And with a green gauze handkerchief
  Wipe the sour sweat away.

Has she gone to Blisland
  To seek an easier place,
And is that why your eye won't dry
  And blinds your bleaching face?

'Take me home!' cried Charlotte,
  'I lie here in the pit!
A red rock rests upon my breasts
  And my naked neck is split!'

Her skin was soft as sable,
  Her eyes were wide as day,
Her hair was blacker than the bog
  That licked her life away.

Her cheeks were made of honey
  Her throat was made of flame
Where all around the razor
  Had written its red name.

As Matthew turned at Plymouth
  About the tilting Hoe,
The cold and cunning Constable
  Up to him did go:

'I've come to take you Matthew,
  Unto the Magistrate's door.
Come quiet now, you pretty poor boy,
  And you must know what for.'

'She is as pure,' cried Matthew,
  'As is the early dew,
Her only stain it is the pain
That round her neck I drew!

'She is as guiltless as the day
  She sprang forth from her mother.
The only sin upon her skin
  Is that she loved another.'

They took him off to Bodmin,
  They pulled the prison bell,
They sent him smartly up to Heaven
  And dropped him down to Hell.

All through the granite kingdom
  And on its travelling airs
Ask which of these two lovers
  The most deserves your prayers.

And your steel heart search, Stranger,
  That you may pause and pray
For lovers who come not to bed
  Upon their wedding day,

But lie upon the moorland
  Where stands the sacred snow
Above the breathing river,
  And the salt sea-winds go.

The poet's introduction tells the reader that 'The Ballad of Charlotte Dymond' is about an actual murder. The poem was written over 100 years after the event. Here is a newspaper report of the murder written just a few days after it had happened. Read it in silence. Then, in pairs or groups, discuss the questions which follow it. Make notes of your opinions and comments. Then report your views to the rest of the class.

DREADFUL MURDER. – On Wednesday an inquest was held before Mr. Joseph Hamley, coroner, and Mr. Gilbert Hamley, deputy-coroner, in the parish of Davidstow, Cornwall, on view of the body of Charlotte Dymond, aged 19. It appeared from the evidence that deceased, accompanied by Matthew Weeks, left her mistress's (Mrs. Peters') house on the 11th inst., about 4 o'clock in the afternoon; they were seen on the moors going towards Roughtor. Weeks returned to Mrs. Peters's house at 9 o'clock, and when questioned as to where Charlotte was, he said he did not know. On the following morning his mistress told him to get up and come and help her, for she was sure he had put away the maid, and he ought to have known better in this busy time. He was repeatedly asked what had become of Charlotte, both by his mistress and some other persons, but he said he knew nothing about her. On the Tuesday following, his mistress said, "I insist on your telling me what has become of the girl." He then said, "If I must tell you, she went to Brown Willy to Caius Spear's house last Sunday, and was going to Blissland the following day, as Mr. Louxon had got an easier place for her." On Friday Weeks said to John Stevens, another servant of Mrs. Peters, "Can you lend me a needle and thread to sew on a button to the collar of my shirt?" Stevens said, "How came your shirt torn? It is almost a new one." He said it was bad sewing. On Saturday Weeks met a man named Bethson, who asked him what he had done with the girl. Weeks said, "I don't know where she is gone, but if she is found murdered, they will take up her mother for it, for she said she would kill her if she came home again." On the Sunday it was suspected that he had murdered the girl, and Mrs. Peters sent Stevens and her son to search the moors. They went to the moors, and traced her patten marks for some time, but shortly lost them. On their return to Mrs. Peters, they found Weeks had put on his best clothes, and run away. As he was leaving, Mrs. Peters said, "Matthew, how have you got your trousers in that mess? You have brushed them so much that the cloth is almost through." He said it was very dirty last Sunday. She begged him to come back to dinner, and he said he would, but he has not been heard of since. On the following day several people went to search for the deceased, and on going down a small bank, they discovered a woman's foot-marks opposite those of a man's, but quite close, as if they had had a struggle. About half a gun-shot from this bank they discovered the body of the poor girl lying on her back, with her throat cut. The wound was eight inches in length, and about two inches and a half in depth. Mr. Good, the surgeon, who made the *post mortem* examination, said it was impossible she could have done it herself, as it was done with such force, that it had partially separated the bones of the neck. When she left home, she had on a bonnet and red shawl, but neither of them have as yet been found, nor have her shoes or pattens. When Weeks went away, Mrs. Peters went into his room, and found his shirt under the bed, with the collar and all the plaits in front torn off. Mrs. Peters examined the shirt the day before the Sunday he put it on; it then wanted no repair, but was a particularly strong one, and almost new. There were also several spots of blood on the sleeve. The jury, without a moment's hesitation, returned a verdict of "Wilful murder" against Matthew Weeks, who was apprehended on Wednesday afternoon, on the Hoo at Plymouth, and immediately removed to Camelford. – *Falmouth Packet.*

THE TIMES, WEDNESDAY, MAY 1, 1844

List the similarities and differences between the newspaper report and the ballad. Think about the following areas:

a   the details of the story
b   the way the story is told
c   the way you feel about the events.

A 'Story song'

Ballads used to be sung by minstrels who wandered from town to town. Ballads are still sung today, not by wandering minstrels, but by their modern equivalent – pop singers!

Below are the words of the song 'Let Him Dangle' by Elvis Costello, from his album 'Spike'. The song is about the hanging of a young man called Derek Bentley, for a killing he did not do. In groups, read the song aloud and if possible listen to the album track as well.

LET HIM DANGLE   Elvis Costello

Bentley said to Craig "Let him have it Chris"
They still don't know today just what he meant by this
Craig fired the pistol, but was too young to swing
So the police took Bentley and the very next thing
Let him dangle
Let him dangle

Bentley had surrendered, he was under arrest,
When he gave Chris Craig that fatal request
Craig shot Sidney Miles, he took Bentley's word
The prosecution claimed as they charged them with murder
Let him dangle
Let him dangle

They say Derek Bentley was easily led
Well what's that to the woman that Sidney Miles wed
Though guilty was the verdict, and Craig had shot him dead
The gallows were for Bentley and still she never said
Let him dangle
Let him dangle

Well it's hard to imagine it's the times that have changed
When there's a murder in the kitchen that is brutal and strange
If killing anybody is a terrible crime
Why does this bloodthirsty chorus come round from time to time
Let him dangle

Not many people thought that Bentley would hang
But the word never came, the phone never rang
Outside Wandsworth Prison there was horror and hate
As the hangman shook Bentley's hand to calculate his weight
Let him dangle

From a welfare estate to society murder
"Bring back the noose" is always heard
Whenever those swine are under attack
But it won't make you even
It won't bring him back
Let him dangle
Let him dangle (String him up)

How does the songwriter emphasise the horror of the hanging in the words and (if you have heard the record) the music?

Here are some more details about the events described in the song.

On the evening of Sunday 2 November 1952, Christopher Craig and Derek Bentley, two teenagers, tried to break into a warehouse in Croydon. They climbed onto the roof and were cornered by the police. Bentley gave himself up, but Chris Craig had a gun and refused to surrender. Shots were fired and Sidney Miles, a police constable was shot dead – 15 minutes after Bentley had been arrested.

In Great Britain during the 1950s, people of 18 and over could be sentenced to death by hanging. Craig was 16, so he was too young to hang. Bentley was 19, so he was old enough. He was sentenced to hang. The Prosecution said that Bentley had encouraged Craig to fire the gun by calling out, "Let him have it, Chris."

At 9 o'clock on the morning of Wednesday 28 January 1953, Derek Bentley was hanged in Wandsworth Prison. As the noose was placed around his neck, and a black hood pulled over his head, Bentley said that he never spoke those five words which had sent him to the gallows.

Here are extracts from two newspapers. One is from the day the death sentence was passed. The other appeared on the morning of the execution.

Evening Standard

39 997   THURSDAY DECEMBER 11 1952   ●●Three halfpence

The verdict: Both guilty of murder

CRAIG TO BE HELD —BENTLEY TO HANG

Jury recommend him to mercy

Lord Goddard tells Craig:

'People not safe while you are free'

Evening Standard Reporter

Christopher Craig and Derek William Bentley were found guilty at the Old Bailey to-day of murdering Police-constable Sidney Miles on a Croydon roof by shooting him. For Bentley the jury added a recommendation of mercy. They were out 78 minutes.

Wearing the black cap, the Lord Chief Justice, Lord Goddard, sentenced 19-year-old Bentley to death. Bentley was taken down.

A MOTHER weeps for her son . . . a sister for her brother. Mrs. Bentley and Iris Bentley, 21, leave Wandsworth Prison yesterday afternoon after a last family visit to see condemned nineteen-year-old Derek Bentley.

But it had not all been tears. Mr. Bentley, who was also there, said: "Derek was cheerful, even under the shadow of the gallows.

"He fired questions at us and asked: 'How are we getting on outside?'

"I told him we were putting up a fight to save him.

"We gave him a photograph of his dogs, a letter from some neighbours and a rosary which someone had sent for him.

"His last words were 'Cheerio Dad, cheerio Mum, cheerio Iris, I will see you tomorrow.'"

Daily Mirror 28.1.53

Now read and listen to the song again. Does having more information about the case help you to understand the song? Do the extra details change the way you react to the song? If so, how?

Ballads and 'story songs' often present a moral or a lesson to be learnt from the story. In a television interview in which he talked about 'Let Him Dangle', Elvis Costello said that the song had a moral.

◆ What would you say is the moral of 'Let Him Dangle'? Do you agree with the song's message?

10

MORE THINGS TO DO

1. In pairs, groups or as a class look at 'The Ballad of Charlotte Dymond' in more detail.

a The story
♦ Why did Matthew kill Charlotte?
♦ Do you feel sorry for anyone at the end of the poem? If so, who? Explain your opinions.
♦ Do you blame anyone for what happened? If so, who and why?
♦ Role play an interview in which Matthew Weeks is interrogated about the murder of Charlotte. One person take the part of Matthew, the others act as the police investigating the crime.

b The rhyme and rhythm
The poem is made up of stanzas of four lines called quatrains. (The word comes from the French word *quatre* meaning four.) The rhyming pattern of the quatrain used in the poem is a, b, c, b. In other words, the second and fourth lines rhyme. This is a very common rhyming pattern for the quatrain and is found in many types of poem, not just ballads.

♦ Can you find any places where the poet has put in some extra rhymes within a line, as well as at the end of lines? In which line of the quatrain does this happen most frequently?
♦ What is the rhythm? (How many stresses, or heavy beats, are there in each line?)

c The sound of words
The writer has made the sound of the words stronger and more interesting by repeating consonant sounds:

'A red rock rests upon my breasts'

This sound effect in a poem is called *alliteration* (see Book One, Unit 11 and Units 11 and 12 of this book). He has repeated vowel sounds also:

'Her Sunday beads among the reeds
Beaming. . .'

The repetition of vowel sounds is called *assonance*.

♦ In pairs, look for some more examples of alliteration and assonance in the poem. Say which sounds are being repeated and how many times they are used. Be careful. Sometimes there is more than one sound involved.

2. See if you can find any story songs which are about real people or actual events. They could be modern pop songs or traditional folk songs. If you can, play and discuss them in class. You could even sing the songs yourself!

2 YOUR OWN BALLADS

The aim of this unit is for you to write a ballad and then read and discuss it with other people.

Here are two ballads written by people of your age. Both were based on newspaper reports, and one of the reports is included for comparison. Read them aloud in pairs, taking a ballad each.

THE DEATH OF SEVEN FISHERMEN   Karen Barlow

Seven fishermen were drowned as fierce north winds swept the East Coast of England. The 33 foot *Carol-Sandra* capsized as her four-man crew attempted to haul in crabpots from heavy seas. Another boat, the *North Wind* went to search for survivors but could find none. The *North Wind* also capsized in high winds. Four of its seven-man crew were saved.

On the East Coast of England
   Gales were rising
While out at sea
   A boat was capsizing.

The boat 'Carol-Sandra'
   Over thirty feet long
In force nine gales
   Sang its swansong.

As it capsized
   Its crew of four
Went down with the boat
   Not far from the shore.

A second boat was sent
   To where the first had been
To search for survivors
   But none could be seen.

The seven-man crew
   Of the boat the 'North Wind'
Were washed off the deck
   By a wave from behind.

A second wave caused
   The boat to capsize
And out of the seven
   Only four did survive.

Helicopters flew in
 As fast as they could
But they couldn't save much
 Try as they would.

The winds have now calmed
 But seven men dead
Consumed by the waves
 Lie on the sea-bed.

O'er the East Coast of England
 The north winds sweep
While back on dry land
 Seven wives weep.

7 die as boats capsize

By Aileen Ballantyne

Seven fishermen were feared drowned yesterday as fierce north winds swept the east coast of England.

The 33ft. Carol Sandra capsized near Flamborough lighthouse as her four-man crew attempted to haul in crabpots from the heavy seas.

Another fishing boat, North Wind, went to search for survivors but also capsized in the high winds. Four of the seven-man crew, including the skipper and his son, were saved.

A helicopter winchman from RAF Leconfield received head injuries during the rescue and had to be detained in hospital.

Wreckage from the Carol Sandra was picked up but there was no trace of survivors.

Four walkers on the cliffs near Flamborough climbed down towards the sea when they saw the wreckage from the Carol Sandra. But their attempt to help ended with them becoming stranded on the rocks. They had to be rescued by helicopter.

The four people missing from the Carol Sandra are Mr Guy Brigham, aged 62, and Mr Peter Brigham, aged 29, of Woodcock Road, Mr Barry Shelton, of Tower Street, and Mr George Gray, of North Marine Road, all in Flamborough. The men missing from the North Wind are all anglers from the Doncaster area.

Ten people are in hospital— four from the North Wind, the helicopter winchman, a life-boatman, and the four stranded walkers.

The skipper of the North Wind, Mr Palmer Cockerill, was recovering with his son David in hospital in Bridlington last night. He told his daughter Janet, aged 25: "the seas were fine and I was gonig up and down looking for survivors from the Carol Sandra. Then we suddenly took four seas at once. They came from nowhere."

Mr Paul Arrow, who saw the North Wind capsize, said: "It was very close under the cliffs. The first wave washed most of the occupants overboard, and the second turned her over."

Karen chose a tragic subject. But ballads do not always have to be tragic as the next poem shows.

THE BACK-SEAT BABY   Paula Card

'Twas early in the morning
And Sheila was in pain
Courageous, though, her husband Clive
To her sweet rescue came.

Into the car they clambered
Outside their Somerset home.
'It all happened so quickly.'
Said Sheila, with a groan.

'You see,' said she, 'it all began
When in the car I stepped.
I felt a twinge inside of me
And from my womb he leapt!'

'A little boy of seven pounds,
A brother for our son.'
'Tell us Sheila: Was it hard work?'
'Not really. It was fun.'

'Over to the husband.
Please tell us what you think.'
'It's all a bit too much for me.
I'm going to have a drink.'

Take heed you pregnant women
All over the world you are
For a quick and easy labour
Go out and buy a car!

MORE THINGS TO DO

Write a ballad of your own. Don't rush into writing, though. Work up to it carefully in stages.

◆ Choose a story
To write your ballad you will need a story. Newspapers are a good source. Look through some newspapers and choose a story that interests you. Most ballads are about tragedies, but the story you choose can be sad or happy. Cut your newspaper story out and bring it to your English lesson.

◆ Become familiar with the details of the story
In pairs or small groups, tell each other, from memory, the story you are using for your ballad. Be as detailed as you can.

◆ Begin writing
Write a first *draft* (rough copy) of your ballad. This may take some time. You should choose a definite rhythm. How many stresses will you use to a line? Will there be the same number in every line, or will the number vary? What rhyme scheme will you use? Will you use 'sound effects' such as repeating consonants or vowels (alliteration and assonance)?

◆ Discuss, check and rewrite your first draft
When you have completed the first draft, read it quietly to yourself to check that it sounds right. Make any alterations that you feel are necessary. Then show it to your teacher and/or to other people in your class. Once your teacher, or a partner, has read it through (perhaps giving you some more ideas, or some suggestions for alteration) go ahead and write the final copy of your ballad.

◆ The final copy
Once you have completed it, read your ballad aloud to your partner, the rest of your group or the whole class. Discuss the poems and your thoughts and feelings about them. Make a display, perhaps including some of the original newspaper reports for comparison. You could even organise a performance of some, or all, of the ballads written by the class for other groups.

REMEMBER
A ballad
◆ tells a story
◆ rhymes
◆ has a regular rhythm
◆ is an oral form of poetry, so the sound of the words is important.

---

3 THIS IS. . .

In the two poems below, each writer gives a list of personal definitions of a general subject. In pairs or small groups, read the poems aloud, and discuss the questions which follow each poem.

BOREDOM   Gareth Owen

Boredom
Is
Me
Gloomy as Monday
Moidering the time away
Murdering the holiday
Just
Sort of waiting.

Boredom
Is
Clouds
Black as old slate
Chucking rain straight
On our Housing Estate
All grey
Day long.

Boredom
Is
John
In bed again
The trickle of rain
On the window pane
And no one
To play with.

Boredom
Is
Trev
Gone for the day
To Colwyn Bay
For a holiday
And me
On my own.

Boredom
Is
My comics all read
The Library closed
Damp clothes before the fire
Deciding
Not to clean my bike
To tidy my room
To help with washing

Boredom
Is
Empty streets
And black telegraph poles
A muddy tractor
On the building site
Shipwrecked in mud

Boredom
Is
A thick circle
Of emptiness
Heaviness
Nothingness
With me
Slumped in the middle

Boredom
Is
Boredom
Boredom is
Boredom
Is
Boredom
Boredom is
Boredom
Is
Boredom
Boredom is
Boredom
Is
Boredom
Boredom is
Boredom
Is
Boredom

Boredom is
Boredom
Is
Boredom
Boredom is
Boredom
Is
Boredom
Boredom is
Boredom
Is
Boredom
Boredom is
Boredom
Is

a Gareth Owen gives a list of his personal experiences of boredom. How does he then deliberately create the feeling of boredom in the reader?
b Could you add any ideas to this list?

LOVE IS. . .   Adrian Henri

Love is feeling cold in the back of vans
Love is a fanclub with only two fans
Love is walking holding paintstained hands
Love is

Love is fish and chips on winter nights
Love is blankets full of strange delights
Love is when you don't put out the light
Love is

Love is presents in Christmas shops
Love is feeling Top of the Pops
Love is what happens when the music stops
Love is

Love is white panties lying all forlorn
Love is a pink nightdress still slightly warm
Love is when you have to leave at dawn
Love is

Love is you and love is me
Love is a prison and love is free
Love's what's there when you're away from me
Love is. . .

a What does this poem suggest to you about love?
b What could 'Love is a prison and love is free' mean?

c Why do you think the poet repeats the phrase 'Love is. . .' at the end of every stanza?

MORE THINGS TO DO

1. In pairs or small groups, choose one of the poems above and practise reading it aloud for a presentation to the rest of the class. You can read the whole poem together, or you can each read one or two lines in turn, or you can use a mixture of the two approaches.

2. Write your own 'This is. . .' poem. You could choose a feeling; for instance you could write your own definitions of boredom, or your own 'Love is. . .' poem; or you could use other feelings such as:

Fear is. . .	Anger is. . .	Disappointment is. . .
Hate is. . .	Frustration is. .	Happiness is. . .

You could use school subjects:

> History is. . .
> Geography is. . .
> English is. . .

Or colours:

> Red is. . .
> White is. . .
> Black is. . .

Or general topics:

> School is. . .
> Illness is. . .
> Friendship is. . .

Here are some hints for writing your poem:

♦ Whichever subject you choose, avoid simply describing it with adjectives, e.g. 'School is boring'.
♦ Don't use general definitions which anyone could write: e.g. 'School is a place where you learn'.
♦ You can use a regular rhyme and rhythm, but it is better to use free-verse.
♦ Organise your definitions into the order which you think is most effective.

REMEMBER
In your poem a general subject comes to life through the individual meaning you give to it with your particular definitions.

---

4 YOU ARE. . .

All the poems below are about people whom the writers knew well. Read them silently to yourself. Then in pairs choose one of the poems to discuss in more detail. What do the images suggest to you about the person described?

YOU ARE. . .   Jo Molloy

You are an open beach
   stretching on with warm sands,
   cool water lapping.
You are a still, airy lunchtime.
You are pale yellow.

You are a mild, hazy smell,
   a cosy, homely house,
but a wide-brimmed, dark blue hat.

You sometimes become a hermit crab
   alone, hiding,
but always there.
You are a productive typewriter,
   communicating information.
You are a shiny piece of copper
   emitting a current of warmth.
But mostly you are a unique everlasting flavour.

YOU ARE...   Kathryn Whitehead

You are a mountain scene,
With snowy peaks and green fields,
With the sun shining down,
And clear blue skies.
The soft colours of a midsummer's sunset.

You are a battered trilby,
Which nobody wants to throw away.
An old welcoming house,
With rafters in the roof,
A larger version of a thatched cottage.
A large noisy printing press,
Almost an antique.

You are a Macdonalds banana milkshake,
A warm yellow colour.
Your smell is yours alone.

You are gold.
You are an otter,
Large, fat, cuddly,
And very contented.

YOU ARE...   Rosanna Travis

You are moonlight guiding me at night,
You are rough and craggy,
Just like a rock, always there.
A bitter aftertaste,
With me night and day.

You are a sweet smell from the valleys,
You are always there, a tiger
Waiting to pounce.
You are fiery red,
The rusty nail in my life.

The Furniture Game

The writers of these three 'You Are' poems used 'The Furniture Game' as a way of developing their ideas.

In 'The Furniture Game' the players think of metaphors for people. When we use a metaphor we say one thing is something else (see Book One Unit 14, Book Two Unit 4 and Unit 8 of this book). The haiku poem on the next page works through a metaphor. What is it?

RABBITS   Wes Magee

Blind panic sets in
and they're off; dodgem cars
gone out of control.

You can play the game for amusement, in groups or as a whole class.
You can also use it as a more serious starting point for writing. Here are
both ways of using the idea.

Version one

♦ Form a circle.
♦ Decide which member of the group will start.
♦ The first player thinks of a person whom the other people in the
  group should know.
♦ The other players try to guess who the person is, by asking questions
  like the following:

What piece of furniture is this person?
What fruit is this person?
What type of weather is this person?

So the game could begin like this:

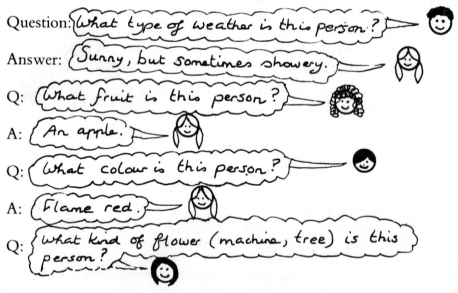

Question: What type of weather is this person?

Answer: Sunny, but sometimes showery.

Q: What fruit is this person?

A: An apple.

Q: What colour is this person?

A: Flame red.

Q: What kind of flower (machine, tree) is this person?

You can set a limit on the number of questions to be asked (e.g. ten) or
you can keep going until the group discovers the answer, and then count
how many questions it took.

Version two, for writing

This version works in a similar way, but this time you write your ideas down.

♦ Decide on ten things that you will use in your 'furniture' questions, e.g. *weather time of day sport garment animal TV programme type of music fruit furniture car flower lesson machine tree*

♦ Everyone thinks of someone famous (e.g. a film star, a pop star, a sports personality, a politician etc.)

♦ Each player in turn asks a question, or one player can ask all ten questions. Pause after each question to write down your answers. Use only a few words.

♦ When everyone has written the answers to the ten questions, take turns to read out your list of metaphors. Start each metaphor by saying 'She (or he) is. . .'

♦ The other people in the group discuss who the famous person could be and how effective and appropriate the metaphors are.

Keep your list of metaphors. You could use it as the basis for a poem.

MORE THINGS TO DO

On your own, do 'The Furniture Game' as a written exercise, using ten objects and thinking of someone you know well, or whom you feel strongly about. You do not need to read the questions aloud. Just write down your answers.

When you have written your list of metaphors, work them into a poem, carefully and in stages.

♦ Read your list again, adding details and lines where you think they are needed.

♦ Organise the lines into two or three stanzas.

♦ Use free-verse. (Do not use a regular rhyme and rhythm.)

♦ Imagine that you are speaking to the person and rewrite the lines adding the words 'You are. . .' either before each stanza or before each line.

♦ Give the final version of your poem a title. (If you wish, this could simply be 'You are'.) Then read your poem to a friend or partner.

5 ASSOCIATIONS

Words are often linked in our minds without our being too aware of it. One word can summon up other words. For instance the word 'blue' might make you think of the word 'sad'. 'Red' might make you think of 'anger' or 'danger'. These words which spring to mind in connection with other words are called *associations*.

The following words have powerful associations. Read them silently and then do the tasks below.

Peace teacher gold red blue sea city war

music autumn heart sun money

Country moon

In silence and with concentration, take each word in turn and make a short list of other words that spring to your mind in connection with it. (Do this quite quickly without rejecting words that you think of automatically.)

Compare lists with a partner. Note the similarities and differences. Then discuss these questions.

a Why might you think of the same words as those of other people?
b Why might you think of different words from those of other people?

Compare your lists in larger groups or as a class. Are there any associations which are shared by many people?

Any Suggestions?

Advertisers often use words which have common, powerful associations to suggest ideas and feelings about their products. Look at the examples on the opposite page.

Discuss these questions with a partner. Make brief notes for a report back to the rest of the class.

a What are the advertisers trying to suggest with their choice of words?
b How do the pictures support the associations being built up with the words?

Delight. The pleasure is mine

A leisurely breakfast of hot buttered toast, smothered in Golden Shred.

Golden roasted, richer, smoother. Nescafé Gold Blend.

The promise of pure gold.

An Ode to Cat Food

The writing below is part of a television commercial for cat food. In pairs or small groups, read it aloud.

GOURMET

'A La Carte' cats
Come in all shapes and sizes
And 'A La Carte' cats
Have many disguises.
But something puts them above
The usual cat race
That's a highly developed
A La Carte taste.

Because Gourmet cats
Have a nose for the good things
That particular taste
A fine cat food brings.
Beef, chicken, salmon –
Those flavours
The truly superior
Gourmet cat favours.

New 'Gourmet A La Carte'
A classic among cat foods.

Discuss the following questions and make brief notes of your answers.

a What is the name of the cat food?
b What is the name suggesting about the product?
c How many times are the words in the name repeated in the poem?
   Why do you think they are repeated so often?
d Which other words or phrases in the poem are strongly associated
   with the name and suggest similar ideas?
e What other poetic devices are used in the poem?
f Is this really a poem, or is it just an advert pretending to be a poem?
   Explain your opinions.

Opposite is the actual television script which was used to make the
commercial. (In places the script is slightly different from the final
wording used in the advert.)

The writing on the left-hand side, under the heading 'Vision', describes
what the viewer sees. The writing on the right is what the viewer hears
at the same time.

Read the script carefully. Pay particular attention to how the vision and
sound of the commercial work together. Some special technical
expressions and abbreviations are used in the script. This is what they
mean:

ECU – Extreme close-up
MCU – Medium close-up
FVO – Female voice-over
Super – superimpose

SCRIPT

Client	NESTLE	*Product*	GOURMET	*Medium*	TV
Title	POEM	*Job No.*	POEM2(S)6	*Draft No.*	8
Length	30 SECONDS	*Date typed*	8/9/88	*ITCA Submitted/Approved*	

Approved: Creative Director _____ *Managing Director* _____

Planning Director _____ *Account Director* _____ *Client* _____

VISION   SOUND

Shot as slow elegant movements in time with the metre of the poem.

Open inside a beautiful "French style" apartment. The camera discovers a smartly dressed woman reading a book of poetry. Quick cut to ECU of a page revealing the poem's title 'Gourmet'. We slowly zoom into her ECU as a white Chinchilla rubs seductively against her legs.

FVO: A LA CARTE CATS COME

IN ALL SHAPES AND SIZES.

Cut to exterior of an elegant country house. The camera tracks along the building revealing a black cat in a window.

Cut to a long shot of a staircase. We see a black cat walking down the balustrade.

Cut to see it walking across a desk covered in Victorian paraphernalia. Cut to ECU of cat's brilliant eyes.

AND A LA CARTE CATS HAVE MANY DISGUISES.

Cut to MCU of Burmilla as he looks around his environment in a very superior manner and sniffs a beautiful vase of flowers.

BUT SOMETHING PUTS THEM ABOVE

THE USUAL CAT-RACE...

Cut to a beautiful white Chinchilla cat as it strolls into the kitchen where we see a woman opening a tin of Gourmet, A La Carte.

THAT'S A HIGHLY DEVELOPED A LA CARTE TASTE.

Cut to ECU of a fork chopping up the food and placing it in a bowl.

Cut to ECU of the white Chinchilla sniffing, eating and enjoying the food.

BECAUSE GOURMET CATS HAVE A NOSE FOR THE GOOD THINGS.

Cut from the white Chinchilla to each of the three other cats (tabby, black and Burmilla) as they eat the three varieties of Gourmet, A La Carte. We see each of them in three different but stylish settings.

THE SUPERIOR TASTE A FINE CAT FOOD BRINGS.

THE BEEF, THE CHICKEN, THE SALMON - THOSE FLAVOURS THE TRULY SUPERIOR GOURMET CAT FAVOURS.

```
Cut to the woman putting down the
book to stroke the Chinchilla cat which
is now relaxing upon her lap.


Super Title:   NEW GOURMET            NEW GOURMET A LA CARTE.
               A LA CARTE.           A CLASSIC AMONG CAT FOODS.

Super Pack:  (Chicken variety)
```

Now discuss these questions.

a How does the vision develop the ideas suggested in the poem?
b How does the rhythm of the TV images work with the rhythm of the words?
c What is the impression of poetry which the advert creates? How does this view of poetry connect with what the advert is suggesting about the product?
d FVO means that a woman's voice reads the poem. Why do you think the advertisers show a woman in the advert and use a woman's voice to read the poem?

MORE THINGS TO DO

1. Look for other advertisements in magazines, on TV or on posters, which use words with powerful associations to suggest ideas and feelings. Make a collection of the words and names you find. Can you spot any words which are often used? Why might this be?

2. Write a poem which advertises a real or imaginary product or place (eg your school) and make this the basis for a television commercial. Write the script of the commercial, which can be serious or humorous, using the professional format shown above. If you have the chance to use a video camera, you could go on to shoot and edit your commercial and play it to other people, asking for their reactions and comments.

6 WORD STREAMS

The poem below is a continuous stream of word associations; a 'word stream' poem. The two 14-year-old girls who wrote it added a rhyme and a rhythm to give the flow of words a sound pattern.

Dress frills bows parties
Cakes biscuits sweets Smarties
Tube London Palace Queen
Jewels crown emerald green
Grass flowers pollen bees
Birds nest twigs trees
Wind gale rain snow
Melt stream water flow
Sea sand buckets pail
Colour white canvas sail
Shop dress ribbon parties
Cakes biscuits sweets Smarties

a What connections and associations can you find between the words in this poem?
b What other pattern have the girls added, apart from the rhyme and rhythm?

With word streams we get rid of the ordinary way of connecting words, in sentences. We use these other links or associations, to create a flow of words.

Here are some more word stream poems by pupils.

Taxi car dragster plane
Road avenue crescent lane
Airship yacht canoe train
Number plate tax disc tarmac drain
Bus bike jeep terrain
Oxcart rickshaw tricycle crane
Road avenue crescent lane
Taxi car dragster plane

Paul Dingley

What is the idea which links all the words in this poem? Give the poem a suitable title.

WEATHER   Jenny Sykes

Rain snow fog hail
Wind storm gust gale
Hurricane tornado breeze blow
Freeze cool sunshine glow
Mist air clouds dew
Snowflakes sleet ice blue
Rainbow lightning water cycle
Condensation vapour icicle

Hospital, born, baby, girl,
Pretty, expensive, jewellery, pearl,
Oyster, sea, water, rain,
Lightning, flicker, hurt, pain,
Glass, clear, reflection, think,
Head, bright, colour, pink,
Flower, grow, baby, girl,
Pretty, expensive, jewellery, pearl.

Caroline Needham

Trace the links in these poems. Sometimes the writer has been ingenious in making the connections. How?
Give the poem a title.

MORE THINGS TO DO

Write your own word streams. Start with an idea, word or phrase and build up a flow of words. Each word should follow on from the previous one.

> **REMEMBER**
> You do not need to use sentences, just a stream of words.
> You arrange that stream of words into a pattern.

7 SHAPE POEMS

For a sentence to make sense, the words must follow one another in a definite order. But in the *shape poems* in this section, the words do not follow one another in sentences. They're all there on the page together, all connected in some way to the subject of the poem, which is suggested by the shape that they make.

Shape poems constantly move and change. You can start anywhere you like and read the words in any order, going up, down, left, right, diagonally – in any direction you choose. Instead of just one poem, there are any number of poems in the single shape, because each time you begin to read the poem you can start in a different place and read the words in a different order, making new connections. So the reader helps to create the poem by choosing the order in which to take the words.

Read the poem below. Then read it again, but this time take the words in a different order. What new connections can you make? What new ideas spring to mind? After you have done that, in pairs discuss the questions which follow the poem.

free
gift jungle
and boom
Still are
children
starving
help blame
Success

Output
jumbo sales
fear share?
get more medicine
money death n
more save life o
Business
big money
British wants a new heart?
ingenuity

a What is this poem about?
b What themes, or repeated words and ideas, can you find in the poem?

Here are some more shape poems written by pupils using word associations. As with the previous example, the words have been cut out from newspapers and magazines, and they've been carefully chosen and placed.

Jackie Lester

Jackie Lester's shape poem suggests a grim story. What is it? She also adds a touch of humour. How?

Dean Foreman

32

Jenny Sykes

Sally Whelan

MORE THINGS TO DO

Try writing your own shape poem, using the following stages:

♦ Collect some newspapers and magazines.
♦ Think of a subject you wish to use for a shape poem.
♦ Very lightly outline your shape in pencil.
♦ Go through the newspapers and magazines and cut out words and phrases which connect with your subject. Do not cut out any pictures; only words. You don't have to look with definite words in mind. Let the words find you.
♦ When you have collected more than enough words to fill your shape, start to fit them in. Choose what you think are the most important and interesting words. This stage is a bit like doing a jigsaw puzzle – don't rush to glue down words as you may want to rearrange them. (You can keep your words quite easily in a small envelope until you are ready to use them.)
♦ When you have finished your shape poem, don't outline it in pen. Let the words make the shape. Try to rub out any of the original pencil marks.

You should end up with a poem which is striking to look at and exciting to read, again and again, in many different ways.

Make a display of shape poems written by the whole class, so that other people can see, read and enjoy them.

8 SIMILES AND METAPHORS

Similes and metaphors are ways of describing things through comparisons (see Book Two, Unit 4). When you make a comparison through a simile or metaphor, you also suggest associations which can be positive or negative, happy or sad, or a mixture of feelings and ideas.

A very famous simile is the start of the poem 'A Red, Red Rose' by the Scots writer Robert Burns:

> 'My love is like a red, red rose
> That's newly sprung in June. . .'

What associations come to your mind from reading this simile?
What do you think Burns wanted to suggest about his 'love' with these lines?

If we rewrite the lines using a different simile we can stir up different associations:

> 'My love is like a green, green nettle
> That's newly sprung in June. . .'

How are these two similes different in the ideas and feelings that they conjure up?

How does the image of the 'green nettle' change the sound and the rhythm? Do these changes alter the impact of the lines? If so, how?

Three Poems
Here are three poems which use similes and metaphors. In small groups, read them aloud. Then discuss the questions which follow them.

This free-verse poem from Africa uses many similes to describe a bull.

THE MAGNIFICENT BULL   Dinka, Africa

My bull is white like the silver fish in the river,
White like the shimmering crane bird on the river bank
White like fresh milk!
His roar is like thunder to the Turkish cannon on the steep shore.
My bull is dark like the raincloud in the storm.
He is like summer and winter.
Half of him is dark like the storm cloud
Half of him is light like sunshine.
His back shines like the morning star.

His brow is red like the back of the hornbill.
His forehead is like a flag, calling the people from a distance.
He resembles the rainbow.
I will water him at the river,
With my spear I shall drive my enemies.
Let them water their herds at the well;
The river belongs to me and my bull.
Drink, my bull, from the river; I am here
to guard you with my spear.

What do the images suggest about the way the speaker in the poem feels towards the bull?

The next poem is from Africa.

THE LOCUST

What is a locust?
Its head a grain of corn; its neck the hinge of a knife;
Its horns a bit of thread; its chest is smooth and burnished;
Its body is like a knife-handle;
Its hock, a saw; its spit, ink;
Its underwings, clothing for the dead.
On the ground – it is laying eggs;
In flight – it is like the clouds.
Approaching the ground, it is rain glittering in the sun;
(Landing) on a plant, it becomes a pair of scissors;
Walking, it becomes a razor;
Desolation walks with it.

a Can you find any metaphors which help to describe the locust? Can you find any similes?
b What do the images suggest to you about the locust?

This final poem uses a mixture of similes and metaphors to turn something as ordinary as a fish into an object of fascination.

TROUT   Seamus Heaney

Hangs, a fat gun-barrel
deep under arched bridges
or slips like butter down
the throat of the river.

From depths smooth-skinned as plums
His muzzle gets bull's eye;
picks off grass-seed and moths
that vanish torpedoed.

Where water unravels
over gravel-bed he
is fired from the shadows
white belly reporting

flat; darts like a tracer-
bullet back between stones
and is never burnt out.
A volley of cold blood

ramrodding the current.

a How many images in the poem can you find connected with guns and artillery?
b What ideas and feelings does this choice of imagery suggest about the trout?
c Do you think the images work well? Discuss your opinions.

MORE THINGS TO DO

Choose something to describe in a series of similes and/or metaphors (eg an animal).

♦ Jot down all the details you wish to concentrate on.
♦ Now think of images to describe them. Consider the ideas and feelings you want your images to suggest. For instance, if you write about a cat you could try to employ images which suggest tameness, or wildness, or both.
♦ Finally, organise the images into a free-verse poem.

Read your finished poem to a partner. What ideas and feelings did your images suggest to your partner? Were they the ones which you intended to suggest? Discuss why the same images might suggest different things to different people.

> **REMEMBER**
> In a simile or metaphor two different things are linked in a comparison. On their own the two objects appear ordinary. Brought together with the power of the imagination, they can be transformed into something new, surprising and even mysterious.

9 'NOVEMBER NIGHT'

Four images have been taken out of the poem below. Fill in the gaps with three effective similes and one metaphor. You can use as many words as you like in each space. (There is no need to write out the whole poem.) Compare your images with those of other people. Look at the complete poem (on p. 94) where you can see the actual images used by the poet.

What other images are used which have not been taken out?
How well do you think they work?

NOVEMBER NIGHT, EDINBURGH   Norman MacCaig

The night tinkles like. . . . . . .
Leaves are glued to the pavement with frost.
The brown air fumes at the shop windows,
Tries the door and sidles past.
onomatopoeia
I gulp down winter raw. The heady
Darkness swirls with tenements.
In a brown fuzz of cotton wool
Lamps fade up crags, die into pits.

Frost in my lungs is harsh as. . . . . .
. . . . I look up, there,
A high roof sails, at the mast-head
Fluttering a grey and ragged star.

The world's a . . . .
It's snug and close in the snoring night.
And outside like. . . . .
The fog unfolds its bitter scent.

38

10 EXTENDED IMAGES

Similes and metaphors usually work as short, single images, but they can also be extended over many lines, even making up a whole poem. The following poem is an extended metaphor.

Read the poem, noticing how the writer develops the central image. Then discuss the questions in pairs.

THE SEA   James Reeves

The sea is a hungry dog,
Giant and grey.
He rolls on the beach all day.
With his clashing teeth and shaggy jaws
Hour upon hour he gnaws
The rumbling, tumbling stones,
And 'Bones, bones, bones, bones!'
the giant sea-dog moans,
Licking his greasy paws.

And when the night wind roars
And the moon rocks in the stormy cloud,
He bounds to his feet and snuffs and sniffs,
Shaking his wet side over the cliffs,
And howls and hollos long and loud.

But on quiet days in May or June,
When even the grasses on the dune
Play no more their reedy tune,
With his head between his paws
He lies on the sandy shores
So quiet, so quiet, he scarcely snores.

a What is the main metaphor in this poem?
b How does the writer develop the image to express different aspects of the sea?
c Is the extended metaphor effective in your view? Explain your opinions.

The key to understanding the next poem also lies in noticing that the various metaphors are all part of the same comparison.

TELEGRAPH POLES   Paul Dehn

These, in the dusk, are bars
  On the lit score of spring,
When early-comer stars
  Lean outward, listening.

Rams to the music muster
  Their horned and tenor herds
Where, on a wire stave, cluster
  The semi-quaver birds.

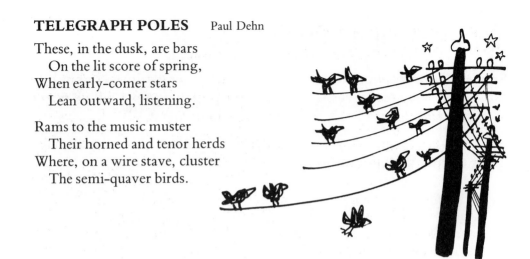

a What metaphor is used to describe the telegraph poles?
b How does the writer develop this image through the poem?
c Do you think the image works well? Give reasons for your answer.

The following two poems were written by pupils who used extended metaphors.

The first poem is inspired by James Reeves' poem 'The Sea' (p 39), but the writer has discovered a different comparison to develop.

THE DESERT   Richard Taffler

The desert is a playful cat
Tormenting the jagged rocks.
In the day he plays a lot,
And his purr
Echoes in the wind.

In the night
His heart turns cold.
Then, as a claw lashed out,
A piercing scream echoes about
And so the night grows old.

Now when he is tired
He takes a bite of rock
Washed down with half an oasis.

His fur, it ruffles in the wind
To form the dunes
We know so well.

What comparison ties the next poem together?

FLOATING DREAMS Vivien Markovic

Lying here
On my bed
Dreams float by
Never stopping
At a port.
When the breeze drops
An occasional thought
Never docking
Pauses and lingers
An Autumn evening
Full of gold and gingers
Images
Of days gone by
But on they voyage
All sails fly
Until once more
The ships come round
Reality lives
My dreams all drowned.

MORE THINGS TO DO

Try to write a poem of your own based on an extended image.

♦ Think of an object or idea.
♦ Note down all the important features and details about it.
♦ Then think of an image which you can connect with your object in a number
  of ways. Below is my example of an extended image.
  What is the basic metaphor in the poem and how effective is it?

BEACHY HEAD Paul Higgins

The sea unfurls
   its white curls
While the wind brushes the sand
   into brown tresses
Over the rocks
   hang the matted locks
      of bladderwrack
And the surrounding hills
   are a patchy scalp
      close cropped and flecked
   with dandruff sheep.

11 ALLITERATION

Alliteration is the repetition of the same consonant sounds (see Book One, Unit 11). Apart from being a musical effect, it can also act as a means of binding words and phrases together in sound to make them more effective and powerful.

Alliteration isn't just used in poetry. In fact it is part of your earliest experience of language. People instinctively use a form of alliteration when they talk to very young babies; some of the first words babies say contain repeated sounds (e.g. Mummy, Daddy).

Alliteration appears all around us: in the titles of books, films, TV programmes and products. Here are some examples:

Who framed Roger Rabbit?   Crocodile Dundee
Postman Pat   Going for Gold   Kellogg's Corn Flakes

Advertisers often use alliteration in slogans because it gives the words more impact and makes them easier to remember:

Bring out the Branston   My mate Marmite
P-P-Pick up a Penguin   Beanz meanz Heinz
You'll never put a better bit of butter on your knife

Alliteration is also used very often in newspaper headlines, so that they pack plenty of powerful punch. In pairs, take turns to read aloud the headlines across these two pages. In each case say which consonant sounds are being repeated. Listen carefully, because sometimes more than one sound is involved.

Nasty Nina's really NICE

COPPE
CAUGH
BY CUFF

Pedal power

BETTING BIG ON BUDDY

Bring on the baffled boffins

Why war-paint woos the warriors from work

Alliteration in a poem

On your own, silently read 'Thistles' by Ted Hughes. Then get into pairs and read it aloud, paying particular attention not only to the sound of the words, but also to the physical movements your mouth and tongue have to make.

THISTLES   Ted Hughes

Against the rubber tongues of cows and the hoeing hands of men
Thistles spike the summer air
Or crackle open under a blue-black pressure.

Every one a revengeful burst
Of resurrection, a grasped fistful
Of splintered weapons and Icelandic frost thrust up

From the underground stain of a decayed Viking.
They are like pale hair and the gutturals of dialects.
Every one manages a plume of blood.

Then they grow grey, like men.
Mown down, it is a feud. Their sons appear.
Stiff with weapons, fighting back over the same ground.

Now turn to page 44

Now turn to page 44

Last
mercy
for
the
Legion
of the Lost

A royal row
rocks the NT

Mugging
for Mr
Money

'Hammy'
hamster
gets the
heave-ho

Britain's
building
bodgers
face big
shake-up

These questions refer to the poem 'Thistles' on page 43. Discuss them in pairs or small groups.

a The writer takes the spiky 'st' sound and repeats it throughout the poem. How many times does this happen? Why do you think he does this?

b Trace the way 's' and 't' sounds are repeated. How do these sounds work with the 'st' sound?

c Pick some other single or double consonant sounds such as 'g' and 'r' (examples of the 'gutturals' mentioned in the third stanza) and trace the way they are used in the poem.

d How would you describe the overall effect of the sound of the poem?

e What images or expressions suggest that thistles and men are locked in a continuing war?

f How does the alliteration in the poem work with this imagery of aggression and battle? How does the sound of the words emphasise the poem's meaning?

MORE THINGS TO DO

1. Collect some examples of alliteration in advertisements and newspaper headlines. Bring them into class and discuss them. As a class, make a collage of your collection for a wall display.

2. Listen to adults talking to young babies. Talk to a baby yourself.

♦ Notice how people often repeat the same sounds. Why do they do this?
♦ In what other ways do adults alter their speech when talking to babies (for example, tone of voice, pace etc.)?
♦ Adults also accompany their words with touching, holding and rhythmical movement of the baby. Why might they do this? How do you think physical contact affects the way a baby experiences and learns language?
♦ Make a tape recording of adults talking to babies. Listen to it and discuss it in class. Are any other 'poetic devices' important in such baby talk (e.g. rhyme, rhythm, repetition etc.)? Can you find any examples of nursery rhymes which use alliteration?

3. Prepare a reading of the poem 'Thistles' for the rest of the class. Concentrate in particular on getting across the strength and force of the words.

12 ALLITERATIVE POETRY

Alliteration isn't just a sound effect that happens here and there in a poem. It can also be used to create a special type of poetry.

Alliterative poetry, like the ballad, is a form of *narrative* poetry – which means that it tells a story. Before the days of printing, very long poems would often be learnt by heart. Alliteration was important because it was an entertaining sound effect which could echo the sounds of the action being described. It also helped the person telling the poem to remember the words.

'Beowulf' and 'Sir Gawain and the Green Knight' are very old poems. Here are two extracts from them, rewritten in modern English by Ian Serraillier.

The Death of Grendel

'Beowulf' was written by an unknown poet (or poets) well over 1000 years ago. Read it aloud in groups; try to bring out and appreciate the effect of the sound.

The story so far
Grendel, a monster 12 feet tall, has been terrorising a place called Heorot, in Denmark, for 12 years. Night after night he murders and devours its warriors. Beowulf, the hero of the poem, has come from Sweden to slay the monster. The people of Heorot hold a banquet to welcome him. Then they all fall asleep, except for Beowulf, who watches. . .

> Over the misty moor
> From the dark and dripping caves of his grim lair,
> Grendel with fierce ravenous stride came stepping.
> A shadow under the pale moon he moved,
> That fiend from hell, foul enemy of God,
> Toward Heorot. He beheld it from afar, the gleaming roof
> Towering high to heaven. His tremendous hands
> Struck the studded door, wrenched it from the hinges
> Till the wood splintered and the bolts burst apart.
> Angrily he prowled over the polished floor,
> A terrible light in his eyes – a torch flaming!
> As he scanned the warriors, deep-drugged in sleep,
> Loud loud he laughed, and pouncing on the nearest
> Tore him limb from limb and swallowed him whole,

Sucking the blood in streams, crunching the bones.
Half-gorged, his gross appetite still unslaked,
Greedily he reached his hand for the next – little reckoning
For Beowulf. The youth clutched it and firmly grappled.
   Such torture as this the fiend had never known.
In mortal fear, he was minded to flee his lair,
But Beowulf prisoned him fast. Spilling the benches,
They tugged and heaved, from wall to wall they hurtled.
And the roof rang to their shouting, the huge hall
Rocked, the strong foundations groaned and trembled.
Then Grendel wailed from his wound, his shriek of pain
Roused the Danes in their hiding and shivered to the stars.
The warriors in the hall spun reeling from their couches,
In dull stupor they fumbled for their swords, forgetting
No man-made weapon might avail. Alone, Beowulf
Tore Grendel's arm from his shoulder asunder,
Wrenched it from the root while the tough sinews cracked.
And the monster roared in anguish, well knowing
That deadly was the wound and his mortal days ended.
Wildly lamenting, away into the darkness he limped,
Over the misty moor to his gloomy home.
But the hero rejoiced in his triumph and wildly waved
In the air his blood-soaked trophy.

That's not the end of the story, because Grendel's monster mother returns for revenge.

a Read the extract again. Note some of the examples of alliteration. Read them aloud to hear their effect.

b How does the alliteration give the events of the story more impact?

The arrival of the Green Knight

The second extract is from 'The Challenge of the Green Knight', an adaptation of the original poem 'Sir Gawain and the Green Knight', which is over 600 years old. (Ian Serraillier has added rhyming couplets which were not there in the original version.) Read it aloud.

The story so far

There have been Christmas celebrations at Camelot, the court of King Arthur. On New Year's Day, the King, his wife Guinevere and his knights are assembled at the banquet table when in bursts a giant knight all in green and carrying a large axe. He insults Arthur and the knights and offers a strange challenge. He says he will take a blow of the axe from one of the knights, if that knight will agree to receive a similar blow from him in twelve month's time. To defend the honour of Arthur and his court, Sir Gawain accepts the challenge.

Then Gawain knelt before the King, took hold
Of the axe, and marched to meet the giant. Bold
And unabashed, he told him his lineage and name,
And agreed to the bond. 'Sir, I solemnly swear
To strike one blow and twelve months hence endure
One blow from you, with any weapon you choose.'
'You have sworn the oath, sir. You cannot refuse!'
The giant cried. 'By God, I'll relish the day
When you come to our meeting-place to receive your pay!'

'But where shall I find you, sir? I neither know
Your house nor your name.'

        'Wait till you've struck the blow.
I'll tell you then.'

        Calmly he knelt down

And bared his neck, tipping over his crown
His long and lovely locks. Gripping the shaft,
Gawain heaved it mightily aloft,
Then whipped it down, severing flesh and bone;
And the blade edge, spurting fire, split the stone.
The head bounced on the floor; like a ball in play,
Kicked from foot to foot it rolled away.

47

But the trunk blood-spattered, neither fell nor faltered;
Though headless, yet – as if unchanged, unaltered –
It strutted along the paving stone still-limbed,
Picked up the head, marched to its horse and climbed
Into the saddle. Then, waving its head on high,
It flashed at Guinevere each ghastly eye.

Slowly the green lips moved and spoke: 'My name
Is the Knight of the Green Chapel, my house and home
In the northern waste. This day, one year ahead,
You must search there till you find me. You took the pledge
Before this company. Be true to it, Gawain.'

With a savage swerve he turned and tore at the rein,
And out he rushed from under the echoing roof,
The head swinging in his hand. Each hoof
Struck fire from the flinty stone as he galloped away. . .
Whence came he? Where was he going? No one could say.

To find out what happens to Sir Gawain, read the rest of 'The Challenge of the Green Knight'.

a What happens in this extract? How does the writer make the events dramatic?

b Look for some examples of alliteration and read them aloud again.

c How many stresses are there in each line?

MORE THINGS TO DO

1 Choose one of the extracts and in pairs or small groups prepare it for a performance to the rest of the class. (See Book Two, Unit 16 for some questions which are useful to think about when you are performing a poem.) Make your performance as dramatic as you can: you could act the poem out, with movements and gestures, props, musical instruments, sound and lighting effects and even costumes and make-up! You could also make a recording of your performance on audio or video tape.

2 Write a poem in which alliteration is the special feature throughout, for example the story of a massive monster, horribly hideous, that's grotesque, gruesome, grimy and grisly.

3 Choose one of the three scenes below and continue the story of 'Beowulf' or 'Gawain and the Green Knight' in alliterative poetry.

◆ While Beowulf is away, Grendel's monster mother comes to Heorot to avenge the death of her son.
◆ Beowulf sets out to find Grendel's mother to put an end to the danger once and for all. She lives in a den under a lake full of monsters.
◆ After the twelve months are up, Gawain arrives at the Green Chapel, deep in the forest. To defend the honour of Arthur and his court, he must keep his part of the bargain and take an axe blow from the Green Knight.

How to Write Your Alliterative Poem

◆ Decide upon a rough outline for the plot of the story.
◆ Decide how many stresses you will have to a line.
◆ Do not use rhyme. This will mean you can concentrate on the alliteration.
◆ Write your first version.
◆ Read it aloud to a partner. Discuss possible changes and make any alterations you think are necessary.
◆ Write the final version.

In pairs or small groups, read out your poems. If you wish, you could perform them, using the suggestions in activity 1.

13 LONG RIDDLES

Long before writing was invented, people made up riddles. They were passed on by word of mouth. Riddles were originally 'dark sayings' connected with charms and magic. To answer a riddle was often thought to mean the breaking of a curse or spell. In many ancient tales, solving a riddle is a matter of life and death for the central character.

Riddles are found all over the world and take many forms. A special type of riddle is the long, or sustained riddle. (*Sustained* means it is kept going.) This is a long description in which the object being described is never named.

The following two examples are very early long riddles, translated into modern English from Anglo-Saxon (a type of very old English). Read the riddles silently to yourself and try to decide what is being described. Then compare your ideas with those of a partner. (If you want a clue, you will find one on page 53).

Translated from Anglo Saxon by Kevin Crossley-Holland

1   Silent is my dress when I step across the earth,
        Reside in my house, or ruffle the waters.
        Sometimes my adornments and this high windy air
        Lift me over the wings of men,
        The power of the clouds carries me far
        Over all people. My white pinions
        Resound very loudly, ring with a melody,
        Sing out clearly, when I sleep not on
        The soil or settle on grey waters. . .
        . . . a travelling spirit.

2   In former days my mother and father
        Forsook me for dead, for the fulness of life
        Was not yet within me. But another woman
        Graciously fitted me out in soft garments,
        As kind to me as her own children,
        Tended and took me under her wing;
        Until under her shelter, unlike her kin,
        I matured as a mighty bird (as was my fate).
        My guardian then fed me until I could fly,
        And could wander more widely on my
        Excursions; she had the less of her own
        Sons and daughters by what she did thus.

The two long riddles below are written by a modern poet, John Mole.
Try to solve them.

3   Through a bright autumnal air
We fall from grace, and from
The arms that held us.

The brilliant discourse of our veins
Has ended now; our fresh green thoughts
Must gossip with the dead ideas
Of yesterday.

Strewn, we lie at your feet
And when disturbed by shuffling children
Know that even they shall not escape.

John Mole

The next riddle is based on an extended image (see Unit 10).

4   We rise, we fall,
Our corporation's global,
Cut-and-thrust executives
From Neptune Inc.

The world admires
Our liquid assets
And the fierce persuasion
Of our fluent tongues.

We overreach each other
In perpetual hurry;
Time is our essence
As the stocks pile high

Then, past the rocks,
Our empire crashes
At the conference table
Of a polished beach.

John Mole

51

Here are some long riddles written by pupils.

5   **SWIFT AS AN ARROW**

Glittering
Gliding swiftly
Among the plants
I was abandoned
Found my way about
Insects scatter
As they see me coming
If taken out
I would die
I'm silver, gold,
Colours of the rainbow
My body plays the scales
As it darts
Hither and thither

6   Pointed and sharp,
See-through pencils are we.
When we're about,
Eaves have fingers,
Window sills eyelashes.
We are like long thin lollipops.
Don't suck us though,
Cold; we are freezing.
Guess our name. We'll give you a go.

7   Thick or thin
Long or short
If it's not washed,
There'll be a terrible smell
And people will go round with noses pegged!
Most children have it,
Some grown-ups do,
If you don't, you look like an egg!
Here's a short cut to this riddle, you see,
Comb every word you find,
And you'll get it, sure as can be.

MORE THINGS TO DO

1. Carry out some research into riddles. Try to discover some ancient examples, and also some stories in which riddles and puzzles are an important part of the plot. Then discuss this question: Why do you think riddles are such a common and lasting form of poetry?

2. Write some long riddles of your own. Pick an object. It could be anything at all which interests you; an animal, a vehicle, a tool, a machine etc. Think of all the details about it, not just the physical characteristics, but the way it moves, sounds and acts. Think about it from every viewpoint, too: above, below, inside, from a distance etc. These questions might help you:

- What can your object do?
- What does it remind you of? What can you compare it with? Can you create any imaginative similes and metaphors for it?
- What colour, shape, texture is it?
- Can you think of any clues which you can give about it, maybe through some sly puns?

On your own, or in pairs, write a long riddle, as if the subject of the riddle is talking about itself. Use free-verse.

Read your riddle to other people for their reactions and comments. Can they solve it?

Clue: Both Anglo-Saxon riddles are about birds.

14 FOUND POETRY

Poems don't just come from inside your head; ideas for poems can be discovered anywhere. What is special about a *found poem*, though, is that the words in it were not originally intended to be a poem, or originally written by the poet who uses them. Found poems are made up of writing or speaking which was already there that the poet has decided to take and put straight into a poem.

The first poem in this unit came about when I caught a girl in one of my English lessons reading the chart shown below from her Science exercise book! I said she could carry on reading it as long as she eventually turned the chart into a poem. I explained what found poems were and she produced the poem 'Food Damage'.

Stopping food damage

Method of Preservation	Effect of Preservative On :				
	Bacteria	Fungi	Oxygen	Water	Acidity
Cooking	kills most types	kills most types			
Chilling	Slows down growth	Slows down growth			
Vacuum Packing	Slows down growth	Slows down growth	Removes and keeps out the gas		
Canning & Bottling	kills all types	kills most types	Removes and keeps out the gas		
Freezing	kills up to 3/4 of all types	Stops them growing		turns Solid	
Dehydration	Stops them growing	Stops them growing		Removes	
Curing	Slows down growth	slows down growth			
Pickling	Makes them inactive	Stops them growing			Makes it more acid
Adding Chemicals	Stops them growing	Stops them growing			May change

FOOD DAMAGE   Lisa Gritton

Bacteria
  fungi
    oxygen
Cooking
    chilling
Kills most types
kills most types

Water
  acidity
    vacuum packing
Slows down growth
slows down
    growth

Canning and bottling
  removes the gas
Kills most types
kills most types

Freezing
  dehydration
Stops them growing
stops them
    growing

Remove the water
  curing
Slows down growth
slows down
    growth

Adding chemicals
  acidity
May change

Pickling
  makes them
    inactive
Stops growth
stops
    growth
    stops.

Look at how the chart is organised. Then carefully compare the poem with the chart to find where the words have come from. In this way you will see how Lisa has used the words on the chart to make the poem. For example, which part of the chart do the first three words come from? Where do the other words in the first stanza appear?

In a found poem you do not use any words of your own except in the title. But you are free to arrange the 'found' material you have chosen in the way that you think is best. *You* make the poem (and not the person who originally produced the writing) because you notice that the words can be used in another way, you select them and you re-present them on the page as a poem.

The writing below was originally part of an advertisement in a magazine, but I decided it could make a found poem:

POUR TOI, THE MEMORY LINGERS ON   Paul Higgins

Softly sensual
   exquisitely feminine
   a total embrace from Tu.
Carefully blended from delicate, oriental spices
   to complement the look of the Tu cosmetic range.

A fragrance
   with just the hint of
Cypress and Patchouli.
Splash it.
Sprinkle a little.
The feeling is beautiful.
All through the day
   and way, way into the night.
Just one tiny drop
   enough to create
   a lingering memory.

Created exclusively for Woolworth.

Do you think this writing can be called a poem? Explain your answer.

Found poems can come from any writing which was not intended to be poetry, eg newspapers, magazines, textbooks, posters, signs, even school desk lids. They can also come from words that people say. The next poem by Michael Rosen is a found poem because he has collected the odd things that parents say and put them together.

PARENTS' SAYINGS   Michael Rosen

You're old enough to wash your own socks.
He's not coming through this door again, I can tell you.
If it's true what your teacher said then you can say
goodbye to the coat we were going to get you.
You do it and like it.
When did you last wash your feet?
Why don't you do a Saturday job?
The answer's NO.
The biscuits are for everyone – O.K.?
Don't mind me, I'm just your mother.
You haven't ridden that bike of yours for years.
You try and leave home and I'll chuck you out on your ear.
You're certainly not going to put that up on any wall in
   this house.
Do you know what a Hoover is?
You can pay for the next phone bill.
If you don't like this caff – find another one.
Just 'cos he's doing Biology he thinks he's going to be a
   brain surgeon.
Do you remember that lovely Christmas when he was six?

Could you add any parents' sayings to this list?
This next found poem is also based on someone's spoken words.

BELT UP   Paul Higgins

Okay. Right.
Pay attention please.
Everybody.
Look, I'm waiting.
If you don't mind.
Look, listen.
Right.
Now today I'd like to. . .
Will you turn round at the back
And face this way?
Thank you.
Look, I don't want to have to
Say this again.
Let's have some quiet now.
Did you hear what I said?
You two stop that.
I don't care whose fault it is.
Just pack it in.

When you're ready.
I'm waiting.
Right. Now.
Look I can still hear
Some people chatting.
When there's quiet
And everyone's paying attention
I can start.
Now as I was trying to say before. . .
Will you
BELT UP?

Who is speaking in this poem? How can you tell?

MORE THINGS TO DO

1. Keep your eyes and ears open for interesting writing or speaking which you could turn into a found poem. Collect some source material which you can plunder for poems, and bring it to your next English lesson. (A cassette tape recorder or a video would be very useful if you want to use speaking, but if you have a good memory, or are good at jotting things down quickly, then you can easily get by without them.) If you are not sure where to look or listen, here are some suggestions for possible sources of found poems:

a set of instructions
a school assembly
a newspaper
an advertisement
a cereal packet
a television programme
the radio
a record sleeve
a travel brochure
a noticeboard
a text book, or
an exercise book

gravestones
a lesson
a magazine
a leaflet
an encyclopaedia
a comic
a wall (graffiti)
a desk lid
a note
a recipe
a card (any kind)

a shop window
a menu
a relative's words
a friend's words
a sauce bottle
a diary
signs
a poster
a letter
a church
a wrapper
(for anything)

How to Write Your Found Poem

♦ Look for and collect source material. At this stage it is best to avoid having fixed ideas about what you want. Keep an open mind. When you have found your words, explore the possibilities and ideas that they suggest to you.
♦ Read the words carefully and decide how they should be arranged on the page.
♦ Give your poem a title. This can be made up of your own words, or 'found' words. It's up to you.
♦ Rewrite the words you have found as your poem.

Compare your found poem with those of other people in the class. You could make a display of found poetry.

58

15 SPEAKING VOICES

The poems in this unit capture the vitality of actual speech. Many of the poems speak in different accents and dialects. To show this, the writers sometimes change the spelling, so that the words sound right.

An *accent* is the way words are sounded or pronounced. A *dialect* is the pronunciation and any special words, expressions and grammar that the speaker might use. Our accents and dialects vary according to our background and where we come from.

Get into pairs or small groups and read the poems aloud to each other. Where poems are conversations between two people, each person in a pair could take a part. Pick one poem to read aloud to the rest of the class. When you have read it say why you chose it and what the poem says to you.

EE SHYNTA DUCKED! Barry Heath

Ken Dado
an
ah Lez
wunt lemme play
an
it want fair
cos
ah ad nobody t'playwee.

an
ah picked up this'ere
building brick
an
said nah can ah play?
an
they said no
so
ah threw this'ere
building brick
an
it smashed Dado's
fruntwinda
an
ah went omm
shatin
'Eee shunta ducked!
Eee shunta ducked!'

FISHERMEN   Anon

Hiyamac.
Lobuddy.
Binearlong?
Cuplours.
Ketchanenny?
Goddafew.
Kindarthay?
Bassencarp.
Enysizetoum?
Cuplapowns.
Hittinard?
Sordalite.
Wahchoozin?
Gobbawurms.
Fishanonaboddum?
Rydonnaboddum.
Igoddago.
Tubad.
Seeyaround.
Yeatakideezy.
Guluk.

When we met I said, 'Where shall we go?'
She said, 'I don't mind.'
I said, 'I don't mind either. Anywhere you like.'
She said, 'I don't know really. What do you think?
I said, 'I don't know.'
She said, 'You say.'
So I said, 'Want to walk?'
So she said, 'Where to?'
So I said, 'I don't know.'
So she said, 'A walk? There's no point in just walking.'
So I said, 'No I suppose not. Shall we just stay here then?'
Then she said, 'No. There's no point in going nowhere.'
So I said, 'Well where shall we go?'
And she said, 'I don't mind. . .'

Michael Rosen

WHA ME MUDDER DO   Grace Nichols

Mek me tell you wha me Mudder do
wha me mudder do
wha me mudder do

Me mudder pound plantain mek fufu
Me mudder catch crab mek calaloo stew

Mek me tell you wha me mudder do
wha me mudder do
wha me mudder do

Me mudder beat hammer
Me mudder turn screw
she paint chair red
then she paint it blue

Mek me tell you wha me mudder do
wha me mudder do
wha me mudder do

Me mudder chase bad-cow
with one 'Shoo'
she paddle down river
in she own canoe
Ain't have nothing
dat me mudder can't do
Ain't have nothing
dat me mudder can't do

Mek me tell you

SIX A CLOCK NEWS Tom Leonard

this is thi
six a clock
news thi
man said n
thi reason
a talk wia
BBC accent
iz coz yi
widny wahnt
mi ti talk
aboot thi
trooth wia
voice lik
wanna yoo
scruff. if
a toktaboot
thi trooth
lik wanna yoo
scruff yi
widny thingk
it waz troo.
jist wanna yoo
scruff tokn.
thirza right
way ti spell
ana right way
ti tok it. this
is me tokn yir
right way a
spellin. this
is ma trooth.
yooz doant no
thi trooth
yirsellz cawz
yi canny talk
right. this is
the six a clock
nyooz. belt up.

The following poems, written by pupils, speak to the reader in a very direct way.

MESISTERSEZ   Leslee Jolley

Mesistersez, Why you got my clip in your 'ead?
Mesistersez, Why you goin' aht wif 'im, 'e's a lowlife
Mesistersez, Wotdyafinkyalooklike?
Mesistersez, Whydontcha 'angyer ironinup?
Mesistersez, Clean up the barfroom!
Mesistersez, You got sum front talkin' ta me like dat.
Mesistersez, Ya wouldn't talk to me like dat if Muvver was 'ere.
Mesistersez, I never smoked at your age.
An' Ah sez, Up yer. . .
Justyooouuwaaiitchasillycow!
Mesistersez.

COURSE I DO   Linda Williamson

Do you still care about me?
Course I do.
You don't love mè though, do you?
Course I do.
Are you sure?
Course I am.
Don't lie to me.
I'm not. I do love you. . but just not as much as. . .you love me.

You're not just saying that.
Course I'm not. Look, what is this?
I'm sorry. It's just that you seem cold to me.
Don't be silly. I love you. You know that.
How do I know?
Why do you think I wanted to go with you Saturday
and why do you think I phoned today? Use your head girl.
Good. I still love you.
Good. And I love you.
That's all right then.
Yeah.
What about tomorrow then?
Oh, well I can't see you tomorrow as I'm working late.
Oh.
Sorry about that.
That's O.K.
Look I'd better go. Bye!
Bye!

In the next poem the writer has combined two ways of speaking in her poem. Read it carefully to follow the various voices involved.

POCKET MONEY   Clare Ward

"This is the BBC six o'clock news."
  Mum shall I make some tea?
"Fighting breaks out on the Afghan border."
  Yes, pour a cup of tea for your dad and me.
"Over eighty villagers already killed in their fight for freedom."
  Dad, can I have my pocket money?
"The drought in Central India continues."
  Ask your mother.
"Food supplies are limited. Thousands die daily."
  Mum, can I have my pocket money?
"Terrorists shoot a policeman dead."
  Why do you want it so early?
"He was married with three children."
  There's a record I want to buy.
"Five people went missing in the Channel last night."
  Wait until Friday. It's only three days.
"There is little hope of finding them alive."
  Oh Mum, I can't possibly.
"A ten-year-old-girl slipped and fell twenty metres from a balcony."
  I want that record now. Why can't I?
"The blow to her head has resulted in loss of hearing."
  IT'S NOT FAIR.

What ideas and connections has the writer developed by combining the voice from the television and the voices of the living-room conversation?

MORE THINGS TO DO

1. Pop and folk songs are sometimes written in a particular dialect. Search for dialect songs . If you have any on record or tape, bring them into your English lesson for the class to listen to and talk about. You could even sing them!

2. Comedians often exaggerate a particular way of speaking to create an easily recognisable character. Can you think of any examples? Make a list.

3. Try to express the energy of actual speech in a poem of your own. Your poem could be based on any of the following ideas:
a conversation   a dialect
the voice of a particular character   a situation (eg the classroom)
the media (eg radio or television)   a contrast between different voices
                                       (as in 'Pocket money' above)
Before you write, listen carefully to the vocabulary, rhythms and mannerisms of the speaking voices you are working on. Read aloud your finished poems.

16 HOT AND COLD DRAFTS

The word *draft,* when used in connection with writing, means a preliminary version of a piece of writing, done before the final copy (see Book One, Unit 8). Drafting is useful in many forms of writing, from stories and plays to essays and letters. In this unit we will concentrate on how it can be used in poetry.

The poet Adrian Mitchell, once described drafting by saying there are two stages to writing poetry: the hot stage and the cold stage. The hot stage is the first draft, when you write the poem without worrying about all the fine details. Spurred on by your imagination, you try to capture the general feeling or idea you have and create the overall shape of the poem. The cold stage is the rewriting, when you come back to the poem and look at it critically, making any changes, corrections, cuts and additions that you think are needed until you have a final version that you are happy with. This could mean more than one draft; you may do a third, fourth and even fifth draft of a poem before you are satisfied with it. (But be wary of changing the original piece so much that all the life goes out of it.)

Before you read on, turn the page. In silence, read 'The Old Tree Stump', a poem by Wes Magee.

'The Old Tree Stump' did not take four or even five drafts to complete. The final version on page 66 is the eleventh draft that the poet produced! On pages 67–70 you can see the drafting sequence, giving a selection of some of the drafts.

Read the sequence to yourself, skimming and scanning to get a general idea of the poem and an overall impression of the way it develops. Then do the tasks which follow it.

THE OLD TREE STUMP   Wes Magee

The old tree stump
is all that remains
of an elm tree
felled years ago.
Now it's our garden seat
comfortably covered
with a moss cushion
upon which our cat
sleeps in the sun.

A dead stump?
Peel back the bark
and see scores of ants
swarming like Londoners
in the rush hour,
or watch the woodlice
trundling like army tanks
to the front line
of some forgotten war.

And here's a centipede
plunging down a crack
like a potholer
exploring unknown caverns.
Later, when we've gone,
a thrush alights
and uses the stump as an anvil
upon which to smash
a land snail's shell.

It's a favourite spot
in our garden,
this old tree stump,
and – you know –
it's quite the best
place to sit
and sun yourself
on a sweltering day
in the middle of July.

Draft 1.

Tree stump life

Ants, red ones,
have populated a country
when you remove a section of bark.
Scores of them run over, into, through,
like London in the rush hour viewed from Space.

Woodlice are also disturbed
when you remove the rotting bark.
They line up, a column of tanks,
then move off to the front line of a war
to take up new positions.

A cat stretches in the day's warmth
on top of the garden stump,
licks its paws, cleans its fur.
A bed of moss grows out of the top.
Beneath it a thousand insects move,
and get on with their lives.

A thrush lands here, on top,
uses the trunk as an anvil to
smash a snail's shell.
Fragments of brown and cream and black,
like a smashed plate or tea pot
telling a tale of violence and hunger.

In the hollow a millipepe cowers,
its red body snaking down into recesses,
a pot/holer going into dark caverns,
caverns which flood when it rains.

The poet added the following stanza at the end of Draft 2:

This tree stump where I sit,
a book in my hand,
a seat for humans while beneath me
creatures go about their lives
perhaps wondering what dark cloud has
blotted out their sun
when I sit down on the tree stump.

Draft 5.

The tree stump in the garden

All that remains of a tree
felled years ago is this stump,
now a garden seat
for a hot day in July.)

And beneath you?
A whole world of insects!
Break off this section
of rotting bark
and see hundreds of red ants
milling like Londoners

in the rush hour,
and here's a line of woodlice
like primitive tanks
trundling off to the front line
in some war or other.   [too vague!]

And at the stump's centre,
where rot has set in,
a hole leads to caverns and passages.   [too much explanation?]
Down plunges a millipede,
a pot-holer lost in the darkness.

When I've gone
a thrush will come and use the stump
as an anvil,
break open a land snail.
The fragments of brown and white shell
lie here
like pieces of pottery
from a broken plate.   repeated "lie"

And our cat will lie
on the stump's mossy cushion,
? sunning and cleaning itself.

For many years it's been a favourite spot,
this tree stump in the garden.

68

Draft 6.

The tree stump in the garden

A stump, our garden seat,
all that remains
of a tall tree
felled years ago.
Now it has grown a moss cushion
across which our cat lies
and suns itself on a warm day.
Much else lives here also:
peel back a section of rotting bark
to reveal hundreds of red ants,
milling in confusion
like Londoners in the rush hour.
And there,
a line of woodlice,

like (primitive) army tanks
trundling off to the front line
of some forgotten war.
And at the stump's centre,
where rot has really set in,
a hole leads to caverns
and passages down which
a pot-holing millipede
plunges into darkness.
And when I've gone
a thrush comes and uses the stump
as an anvil to smash open
a land snail.
See the fragments of shell
like pieces of brown and white
pottery from a broken plate.
A favourite place,
this stump.
No better place to sit
on a hot day in July.

Draft 8.

The old tree stump

The tree stump,
all that remains
of a tall tree
felled years ago,
and now its our garden seat
with a cushion of green moss
on which our cat lies,
sunning itself.

A dead tree stump?
Hardly. So much lives here.
Peel back rotting bark
and reveal hundreds ——— *scores*
of red ants
milling like Londoners   *Swarming*
in the rush hour.

And there, see woodlice.
They motor off like
primitive tanks   *?*
heading for the front line
of some forgotten war.

And in the stump's centre
is a hole down which
a millipede potholes,
plunges at high speed   *explore*
to dark caverns   *unknown ?*
and passages far below.

A thrush, too, visits.
Using the stump as an anvil
it smashes a land snail's shell.
Fragments lie like pottery   *leave out*
from a broken plate.

It's a favourite spot
in the garden,
and there's no better place
to be on a hot day   *sweltering*
in the middle of July.

70

In pairs or small groups, choose any two of the drafts shown above, including the final version, and read them carefully. Study and discuss them in detail, using these questions as a starting point:

a What changes have been made between the two drafts you have chosen?

b Pick three or four changes and try to suggest reasons the poet could have had for making them. Do you agree with the poet's decisions? Are the alterations always an improvement?

c Using three or four examples, suggest some alternative changes of your own which you think could have worked.

d Report back to the rest of the class about the two drafts you worked on.

Wes Magee has provided a commentary which tells the story of how the poem took its final form. Compare his explanation of the various stages of the poem, and the changes he made to it, with what you discovered about it in your close reading and discussion.

Commentary

Some years ago a large elm tree was felled in my back garden. The stump became a natural seat, a pleasant place to sit in summer. However, as the years passed the stump weathered and it became home to many insects. Fungi and moss and weeds grew as the wood softened and rotted. The stump was attacked relentlessly by the weather season **after season.**

What **looked,** at first glance, a static, dead stump was in fact crammed with life forms. It seemed worthwhile recording such observation in a poem. My first draft, written 'on site', was a list of things I saw when I looked closely at the stump.

The second draft, written immediately after, merely improved the observations set out in draft 1. I added a

final section (or stanza) so bringing <u>myself</u> into
the poem. I was a user of the stump, just like the
ants, the woodlice, the thrush.

By Draft 5 I was beginning to tighten the sections of
description. Even so the poem had grown longer! There
wasn't a great deal of structure or shape yet I did
manage to find a satisfactory last line for the poem.
The title also was becoming more definite.

The next draft (number 6) found me squashing the entire
poem into one, unbroken stanza. Generally the lines
became shorter as I pared away and **tightened** up my
writing. Padding was discarded. The poem took on a
leaner and fitter look. It was now moving towards
a properly completed, and polished, object.

Throughout drafts 7 and 8 I returned to stanza breaks
and the line lengths grew more regular. By draft 8 the
'running order' of the poem became firm, and it was
then a matter of refining and polishing. The final <u>shape</u>
of the poem is an important factor and it adds to the
overall impression the poem creates in the mind, and the
eye, of the reader.

Finally, at draft 11, the poem was complete. I ended up
with four stanzas, each with 9 lines. The line lengths
were natural, and I wanted them to read easily and without
'strain'. This, I hoped, would help to create a feeling
of warmth and relaxation.....like sitting in a garden
on a hot day.

> Does having this information help you to understand and appreciate the
> poem more fully? Or does it make the poem less interesting and
> enjoyable? Explain your views.

Using Computers

A computer gives different possibilities for drafting a piece of writing. This is because corrections and alterations are very easy to make, and also because the changes you wish to make don't have to happen in definite drafts, as they did with Wes Magee's poem. Drafting becomes a continuous process – something which is happening all the time.

Nevertheless, it is a good idea to keep various versions of a poem, in case you change your mind about alterations you make, and because you will be able to look back and see how your poem developed.

The idea of poetry writing as a continuous process of choosing, changing, decision-making and building, leads to another big question: *How do you know when a poem that you are writing is finished?*

Discuss this question in groups or as a class.

MORE THINGS TO DO

Write a poem about anything you like. Your teacher will give you a list of themes, or you can read some poems in the Anthology for inspiration. Work up to the final version in a number of drafts. The following plan will be useful for writing your poem.

- When you have an idea, jot down – in any order – all the words, thoughts and feelings that come into your mind in connection with your subject. Then think about the form of poem which will best suit your subject and what you want to say; for example a ballad, a limerick, free-verse, haiku etc.
- Write your first draft (the hot stage).
- Then work on it (the cold stage) until you're satisfied with it. This could mean a number of drafts. Also, the cold stage isn't necessarily something which you complete on your own. It could mean discussing your writing with other people, such as friends, parents, teachers, relatives, and then making changes in the light of their comments.
- Keep the various drafts so that you can compare them with your final version. If possible, put all the versions together in your book or on the wall to show how you came to write your poem and the work you did.
- Write a commentary which tells how your poem developed and the thinking behind the changes you made.

REMEMBER
Working hot and cold like this, you are more likely to achieve an effective piece of writing and to create a poem with its own life.

AN ANTHOLOGY

An anthology is a collection of poems. This anthology contains poems for further reading, work and enjoyment. But this collection is only my choice. As time goes on you can choose your own poems and make up your own anthology. You can do this either just by writing down the titles of the poems you like (and the titles of the books where you found them) at the back of your exercise book, or in a notebook, or you can have a special exercise book in which you copy out poems that you like, to keep and to read in the future. Then, in time, you will have your own anthology which you will be able to read and enjoy and which might also tell you something about yourself. So keep your eyes, ears and minds open, because you can find poems anywhere.

Contents

DAILY LONDON RECIPE

Take any number of them
you can think of,
pour into empty red bus
      until full,
and then push in
      ten more.

Allow enough time
to get hot under the collar
before transferring into
multistorey building.
Leave for eight hours,
and pour back into same bus
      already half full.
      Scrape remainder off.

When settled down
tip into terraced houses each
carefully lined with copy of
The Standard Tit Bits.
Place mixture before open
television screen at 7 p.m.
and then allow to cool
in bed at 10.30 p.m.
May be served with
working overalls
or pinstripe suit.

Steve Turner

THE WARM AND THE COLD

Freezing dusk is closing
    Like a slow trap of steel
On trees and roads and hills and all
    That can no longer feel.
        But the carp is in its depth
           Like a planet in its heaven.
        And the badger in its bedding
           Like a loaf in the oven.
        And the butterfly in its mummy
           Like a viol in its case.
        And the owl in its feathers
           Like a doll in its lace.

Freezing dusk has tightened
    Like a nut screwed tight
On the starry aeroplane
    Of the soaring night.
        But the trout is in its hole
           Like a chuckle in a sleeper.
        The hare strays down the highway
           Like a root going deeper.
        The snail is dry in the outhouse
           Like a seed in a sunflower.
        The owl is pale on the gatepost
           Like a clock on its tower.

Moonlight freezes the shaggy world
    Like a mammoth of ice-
The past and the future
    Are the jaws of a steel vice.
        But the cod is in the tide-rip
           Like a key in a purse.
        The deer are on the bare-blown hill
           Like smiles on a nurse.
        The flies are behind the plaster
           Like the lost score of a jig.
        Sparrows are in the ivy-clump
           Like money in a pig.

Such a frost
   The flimsy moon
      Has lost her wits.

      A star falls.

The sweating farmers
   Turn in their sleep
      Like oxen on spits.

Ted Hughes

CLASS ADS

SWAP? SELL? SMALL ADS SELL FAST

1950 Dad. Good runner; needs one or
Two repairs; a few grey hairs but
Nothing a respray couldn't fix
Would like a 1966 five speed turbo
In exchange: something in the sporty
Twin-carb range.

1920s Granny. Not many like this
In such clean and rust free state.
You must stop by to view! All chrome
As new, original fascia retained
Upholstery unstained. Passed MOT
Last week: will only swap for some-
Thing quite unique.

1990 low mileage Brother. As eco-
Nomical as any other. Must mention
Does need some attention. Stream-
Lined, rear spoiler. Runs on milk
Baby oil and gripe water. Serviced;
Needs rear wash/wipe. Only one
Owner; not yet run in. Will swap
For anything.

Trevor Millum

SUNKEN EVENING

The green light floods the city square –
   A sea of fowl and feathered fish,
   Where squalls of rainbirds dive and splash
And gusty sparrows chop the air.

Submerged, the prawn-blue pigeons feed
   In sandy grottoes round the Mall,
   And crusted lobster-buses crawl
Among the fountains' silver weed.

There, like a wreck, with mast and bell,
   The torn church settles by the bow,
   While phosphorescent starlings stow
Their mussel shells along the hull.

The oyster-poet, drowned but dry,
   Rolls a black pearl between his bones;
   The typist, trapped by telephones,
Gazes in bubbles at the sky.

Till, with the dark, the shallows run,
   And homeward surges tide and fret –
   The slow night trawls its heavy net
And hauls the clerk to Surbiton.

Laurie Lee

FULL HOUSE

Words inhabit my head
like a house. In over-
enthusiasm they tumble
downstairs in a jumble
of arms and legs and
syllables. Some words
shout at me, waving
banners of grammar
from attic windows.

Some I find sitting
prim as sentences
on the settee. Others
hide in cupboards,
come out confused,
complicated as cross-
words. The lazy ones
won't get out of bed
in the mornings, lie

and wait for me to
rouse them thought
by thought. They
ignore me altogether
at times, carry on
as if I wasn't there,
whisper in corners
upsetting my ideas.

Sometimes words rebel,
won't rock to my rhythms,
move meanings around
like furniture. Mostly
they keep busy polishing
their phrases. At night
they run from room to
room scripting my dreams.

Moira Andrew

ALTERNATIVE ENDINGS TO AN UNWRITTEN BALLAD

I stole through the dungeons, while everyone slept,
    Till I came to the cage where the Monster was kept.
There, locked in the arms of a Giant Baboon,
    Rigid and smiling, lay . . . MRS RAVOON!

I climbed the clock-tower in the first morning sun
    And 'twas midday at least ere my journey was done;
But the clock never sounded the last stroke of noon,
    For there, from the clapper, swung MRS RAVOON.

I hauled in the line, and I took my first look
    At the half-eaten horror that hung from the hook.
I had dragged from the depths of the limpid lagoon
    The luminous body of MRS RAVOON.

I fled in the tempest, through lightning and thunder,
    And there, as a flash split the darkness asunder,
Chewing a rat's-tail and mumbling a rune,
    Mad in the moat squatted MRS RAVOON.

I stood by the waters so green and so thick,
    And I stirred at the scum with my old, withered stick;
When there rose through the ooze, like a monstrous balloon,
    The bloated cadaver of MRS RAVOON.

Facing the fens, I looked back from the shore
    Where all had been empty a moment before;
And there, by the light of the Lincolnshire moon,
    Immense on the marshes, stood . . . MRS RAVOON!

Paul Dehn

METAPHORS

I'm a riddle in nine syllables
An elephant, a ponderous house,
A melon strolling on two tendrils.
O red fruit, ivory, fine timbers!
This loaf's big with its yeasty rising.
Money's new minted in this fat purse.
I'm a means, a stage, a cow in calf.
I've eaten a bag of green apples,
Boarded the train there's no getting off.

Sylvia Plath

BEAUTY

Beauty
is a fat black woman
walking the fields
pressing a breezed
hibiscus
to her cheek
while the sun lights up
her feet

Beauty
is a fat black woman
riding the waves
drifting in happy oblivion
while the sea turns back
to hug her shape

Grace Nichols

NOT WAVING BUT DROWNING

Nobody heard him, the dead man,
But still he lay moaning:
I was much further out than you thought
And not waving but drowning.

Poor chap, he always loved larking
And now he's dead
It must have been too cold for him his heart gave way
They said.

Oh no no no, it was too cold always
(Still the dead one lay moaning)
I was much too far out all my life
And not waving but drowning.

Stevie Smith

BEHIND THE WALL   Tracy Chapman – Vocal

Last night I heard the screaming
Loud voice behind the wall
Another sleepless night for me
It won't do no good to call
The police
Always come late
If they come at all

And when they arrive
They say they can't interfere
With domestic affairs
Between a man and his wife
And as they walk out the door
The tears well up in her eyes

Last night I heard the screaming
Then a silence that chilled my soul
I prayed that I was dreaming
When I saw the ambulance in the road

And the policeman said
"I'm here to keep the peace
Will the crowd disperse
I think we all could use some sleep"

Tracy Chapman

TALK WAR

Talk war
War love
Love touch
Touch peace
Peace beat
Beat slip
Slip waste
Waste hate
Hate take
Take slice
Slice break
Break limbs
Limbs play
Play pain
Pain joy
Joy caress
Caress ploy
Ploy plan
Plan flight
Flight light
Light middle
Middle hand
Hand Wave
Wave ocean
Ocean land
Land walk
Walk destroy
Destroy War
War talk
Talk stop
Stop learn
Learn to
To breathe
Breathe love
Love touch
Touch peace
Peace.

Albie Olivierre

MOUNTAIN LION

Climbing through the January snow, into the Lobo Canyon
Dark grow the spruce-trees, blue is the balsam, water sounds
    still unfrozen, and the trail is evident.

Men!
Two men!
Men! The only animal in the world to fear!

They hesitate.
We hesitate.
They have a gun.
We have no gun.

Then we all advance, to meet.

Two Mexicans, strangers, emerging out of the dark and snow
    and inwardness of the Lobo valley.
What are they doing here on this vanishing trail?

What is he carrying?
Something yellow.
A deer?

Qué tiene, amigo?
León –

He smiles, foolishly, as if he were caught doing wrong.
And we smile, foolishly, as if we didn't know.
He is quite gentle and dark-faced.

It is a mountain lion,
A long, long slim cat, yellow like a lioness.
Dead.

He trapped her this morning, he says, smiling foolishly.

Lift up her face,
Her round, bright face, bright as frost.
Her round, fine-fashioned head, with two dead ears;
And stripes in the brilliant frost of her face, sharp, fine dark rays,
Dark, keen, fine rays in the brilliant frost of her face.
Beautiful dead eyes.

Hermoso es!

They go out towards the open;
We go on into the gloom of Lobo.
And above the trees I found her lair,
A hole in the blood-orange brilliant rocks that stick up, a little cave.
And bones, and twigs, and a perilous ascent.

So, she will never leap up that way again, with the yellow flash
  of a mountain lion's long shoot!
And her bright striped frost-face will never watch any more, out
  of the shadow of the cave in the blood-orange rock,
Above the trees of the Lobo dark valley-mouth!

Instead, I look out.
And out to the dim of the desert, like a dream, never real;
To the snow of the Sangre de Cristo mountains, the ice of the
  mountains of Picoris,
And near across at the opposite steep of snow, green trees
  motionless standing in snow, like a Christmas toy.

And I think in this empty world there was room for me and a
  mountain lion.
And I think in the world beyond, how easily we might spare a
  million or two of humans
And never miss them.
Yet what a gap in the world, the missing white frost-face of that
  slim yellow mountain lion!

D.H. Lawrence

85

MEN TALK
(Rap)

Women
Rabbit rabbit rabbit women
Tattle and titter
Women prattle
Women waffle and witter

Men Talk. Men Talk.

Women into Girl Talk
About Women's Trouble
Trivia 'n' Small Talk
They yap and they babble

Men Talk. Men Talk.

Women yatter
Women chatter
Women chew the fat, women spill the beans
Women aint been takin'
The oh-so Good Advice in them
Women's Magazines

A Man Likes A Good Listener.

Oh Yeah
I like A Woman
Who likes me enough
Not to nitpick
Not to nag and
Not to interrupt 'cause I call that treason
A woman with the Good Grace
To be struck dumb
By me Sweet Reason. Yes—

A Man Likes a Good Listener

A Real
Man
Likes a Real Good Listener
Women yap yap yap
Verbal Diarrhoea is a Female Disease
Woman she spread rumours round she
Like Philadelphia Cream Cheese.

                    Oh
        Bossy Women Gossip
        Girlish Women Giggle
    Women natter, women nag
    Women niggle niggle niggle

            Men Talk.

                Men
        Think First, Speak Later
            Men Talk.

            Liz Lochhead

LEVIATHAN

You can't make whales
Make whales.
Hens don't seem to mind
Laying eggs for you.
The patient cow
Conceives at the squirt of a syringe.
Shoals of fry
Will populate concrete ponds,
But whales cannot be handled
Contained
Farmed
Made familiar like dolphins or lions
Herded like pigs or sheep.
Their procreation is their own affair
Their milk for their own young.
In death only does man
Find them valuable.

When none are left
Their monumental bones
Will stand stripped in museums,
The pictures wonderful on the page
At W in a child's alphabet,
Like D for Dodo,
H for humanity.

Pamela Gillilan

CARDINAL IDEOGRAMS

0   A mouth. Can blow or breathe,
be funnel, or Hello.

1   A grass blade or a cut.

2   A question seated. And a proud
bird's neck.

3   Shallow mitten for two-fingered hand.

4   Three-cornered hut
on one stilt. Sometimes built
so the roof gapes.

5   A policeman. Polite.
Wearing visored cap.

6   O unrolling,
tape of ambiguous length
on which is written the mystery
of everything curly.

7   A step,
detached from its stair.

8   The universe in diagram:
A cosmic hourglass.
(Note enigmatic shape,
absence of any valve of origin,
how end overlaps beginning.)
Unknotted like a shoelace
and whipped back and forth,
can serve as a model of time.

9   Lorgnette for the right eye.
In England or if you are Alice
the stem is on the left.

10   A grass blade or a cut
companioned by a mouth.
Open? Open. Shut? Shut.

May Swenson

THE FLOWERS

After lunch my daughter picked
handfuls of the wild flowers
she knew her grandfather liked best
and piled them in the basket of her bicycle,
beside an empty jam-jar and a trowel;
then, swaying like a candle-bearer,
she rode off to the church
and, like a little dog, I followed her.

She cleared the grave of nettles
and wild parsley, and dug a shallow hole
to put the jam-jar in. She arranged
the flowers to look their best
and scraped the moss from the stone,
so you could see whose grave
she had been caring for.
It didn't take her long – no longer
than making his bed in the morning
when he had got too old to help her.

Not knowing how to leave him,
how to say good–bye, I hesitated
by the rounded grave. *Come on,*
my daughter said, *It's finished now.*
And so we got our bicycles and rode home
down the lane, moving apart
and coming together again,
in and out of the ruts.

Selina Hill

TONIGHT AT NOON

★ (For Charles Mingus and the Clayton Squares)

Tonight at noon
Supermarkets will advertise 3d EXTRA on everything
Tonight at noon
Children from happy families will be sent to live in a home
Elephants will tell each other human jokes
America will declare peace on Russia
World War I generals will sell poppies in the streets on November 11th
The first daffodils of autumn will appear
When the leaves fall upwards to the trees

Tonight at noon
Pigeons will hunt cats through city backyards
Hitler will tell us to fight on the beaches and on the landing fields
A tunnel full of water will be built under Liverpool
Pigs will be sighted flying in formation over Woolton
and Nelson will not only get his eye back but his arm as well
White Americans will demonstrate for equal rights
in front of the Black House
and the Monster has just created Dr Frankenstein

Girls in bikinis are moonbathing
Folksongs are being sung by real folk
Artgalleries are closed to people over 21
Poets get their poems in the Top 20
Politicians are elected to insane asylums
There's jobs for everyone and nobody wants them
In back alleys everywhere teenage lovers are kissing
in broad daylight
In forgotten graveyards everywhere the dead will quietly
bury the living
and
You will tell me you love me
Tonight at noon

Adrian Henri

★ The title for this poem is taken from an LP by Charles Mingus, *Tonight at Noon*,
Atlantic 1416

MY BOX

My box is made of golden oak,
my lover's gift to me.
He fitted hinges and a lock
of brass and a bright key.
He made it out of winter nights,
sanded and oiled and planed,
engraved inside the heavy lid
in brass, a golden tree.

In my box are twelve black books
where I have written down
how we have sanded, oiled and planed,
planted a garden, built a wall,
seen jays and goldcrests, rare red kites,
found the wild heartsease, drilled a well,
harvested apples and words and days
and planted a golden tree.

On an open shelf I keep my box.
Its key is in the lock.
I leave it there for you to read,
or them, when we are dead,
how everything is slowly made,
how slowly things made me,
a tree, a lover, words, a box,
books and a golden tree.

Gillian Clarke

THE TELEVISION POEM

(For Patrick Taggart)

It is midnight.
You are passing the window
of a television showroom –
the door is barred,
a wire grille is in the window.
The shop is closed.

This poem is being transmitted to you
from inside the television showroom.
This poem comes to you twice in colour,
twice in black and white.
This poem is 625 line.
This poem is 21 inches
across the diagonal.

You do not hear this poem –
for all you know
this poem could be forecasting ice.
This poem could be telling of the world's end,
this poem could, conceivably,
be singing.

You will see this poem
but will fail to recognise it.
You will not hear this poem
without straining to hear it.
This poem is a mouth opening and closing
and opening and closing
and opening. O.

This poem is subliminal –
dismiss it.
This poem is ephemeral
and eminently passable.
Pass this poem –
let the poem be.

This poem is not for you.
This is my poem,
it is private.
Do not halt in your tracks for this poem.
Go about your business.
See her home.
See yourself home.

You will go home, together or alone.
You will sleep, together or alone.
In the morning you will awaken
and will forget every word of this poem.
There is nothing to remember.
There is nothing to forget.

You will not hear this poem.
This happens to most poems.

Pete Morgan

ACCORDING TO MY MOOD

I have a poetic licence, i WriTe thE way i waNt.
i drop my full stops where i like. . . . .
MY CAPITAL LeteRs go where i liKE,
i order from MY PeN, i verse the way i like (i do my spelling
    write)
Acording to my MOod.
i HAve poetic licence,
i put my comments where i like,,((()).
(((my brackets are write((
I REPEAT WHen i likE.
i can't go rong,
i look and i.c.
It's rite.
i REpeat when i liKE. i have
poetic licence!
don't question me????

Benjamin Zephaniah

This is the original version of the poem you completed on page 38.

NOVEMBER NIGHT, EDINBURGH   Norman MacCaig

The night tinkles like ice in glasses.
Leaves are glued to the pavement with frost.
The brown air fumes at the shop windows,
Tries the door and sidles past.

I gulp down winter raw. The heady
Darkness swirls with tenements.
In a brown fuzz of cotton wool
Lamps fade up crags, die into pits.

Frost in my lungs is harsh as leaves
Scraped up on paths. I look up, there,
A high roof sails, at the mast-head
Fluttering a grey and ragged star.

The world's a bear shrugged in his den.
It's snug and close in the snoring night.
And outside like chrysanthemums
The fog unfolds its bitter scent.

Answers to the long riddles in Unit 13.

1. Swan
2. Cuckoo
3. Leaves
4. Waves
5. A fish
6. Snow
7. Icicles
8. Hair

Book List

If you would like to read more poems by any of the writers named in this book, then here is a list of authors and titles for you to explore. But remember, no list of writers is ever complete. There are many other books of poems on the shelf, just waiting to be discovered – by you!

Secret Destinations, Figure of 8 Narrative Poems, Figgie Hobbin and *Collected Poems,* Charles Causley, Macmillan

Stories in Verse edited by Charles Causley, Batsford

Collected Poems, Gillian Clarke, Carcanet

Death of a Naturalist, Selected Poems 1965–75, Seamus Heaney, Faber and Faber

Collected Poems, Adrian Henri, Allison and Busby

Saying Hello at the Station, Selina Hill, Chatto and Windus

The Hawk in the Rain, Lupercal, Wodwo, Season Songs, Selected Poems 1957–67, Selected Poems 1957–81, Ted Hughes, Faber and Faber

The Complete Poems, D.H. Lawrence, Laurence Pollinger Ltd and the estate of Mrs Frieda Lawrence

Dreaming Frankenstein, Collected Poems, True Confessions and *New Clichés* Liz Lochhead, Polygon Books

The Sinai Sort and *Surroundings,* Norman MacCaig, The Hogarth Press Ltd.
Collected Poems, Norman MacCaig, Chatto

Morning Break and Other Poems Wes Magee, Cambridge University Press

No Man's Land, Wes Magee, Blackstaff Press

The Grey Mare Being the Better Steed, The Spring Collection, A Winter Visitor, Pete Morgan, Secker and Warburg

The Fat Black Woman's Poems Grace Nichols, Virago

The Colossus, Crossing the Water, Winter Trees, Ariel, Sylvia Plath, Faber and Faber

New and Collected Poems, Vernon Scannell, Pergamon

Beowulf the Warrior, The Challenge of the Green Knight, Ian Serraillier, Oxford University Press

I'll Tell You a Tale Ian Serraillier, Puffin and Kestrel Books

Collected Poems, Stevie Smith, Penguin Modern Classics

To Mix with Time, May Swenson, Charles Scribner

Collected Poems, May Swenson, André Deutsch Ltd

The Dread Affair, Benjamin Zephaniah, Century Hutchinson

Anthologies:

A Choice of Anglo-Saxon Verse, Edited and translated by R. Hamer, Faber and Faber

The Faber Book of Ballads, Edited by Matthew Hodgart, Faber and Faber

Caribbean Poetry Now Edited by Steven Brown, Hodder and Stoughton

It is also worth looking at the lyrics of some songwriters in more detail. 'Let Him Dangle' comes from Elvis Costello's LP 'Spike' (Warner Brothers). His other albums include:

My Aim Is True	Stiff
Get Happy!!	F–Beat
Punch the Clock	F–Beat
Blood and Chocolate	Imp–Demon

The words and music to many of his songs can be found in the following two song books:

Elvis Costello – A Singing Dictionary   Plangent Visions
Elvis Costello – Everyday I Write the Song (Grumbling Appendix to the Singing Dictionary)   Plangent Visions

'Behind the Wall' is on the album 'Tracy Chapman' Tracy Chapman Elektra/Asylum Records.